RAILWAYS IN NORTH LINCOLNSI

Chris Bates and Martin Bairstow

Class B1 4 – 6 – 0 No 61408 setting off from New Holland Pier with a local for Cleethorpes in June 1957.
(Peter Sunderland)

Published by Martin Bairstow, 53 Kirklees Drive, Farsley, Leeds
Printed by The Amadeus Press, Cleckheaton, West Yorkshire

Introduction

The lines covered by this book comprise broadly the former Great Central Railway east of Doncaster, east of Retford and north of Lincoln. The GN/ GE Joint Line between Gainsborough and Lincoln is included because its story is inseparable from that of the Great Central. The NE/ L&Y Axholme Joint is included because it penetrated the area. We also include the Great Grimsby Street Tramways and, from later eras, the Lincolnshire Coast and Cleethorpes Coast Light Railways.

The Railway built the docks at both Grimsby and Immingham. The latter project was a bold step, which nearly crippled the Great Central financially. Yet today, Immingham is the country's busiest port and biggest source of rail freight traffic. We look both historically at the Great Central's steamer services to the Continent and, more up to date, at today's enterprise at Immingham.

We are grateful to everybody who has helped with the book. The photographs are credited individually. John Foreman drew the signal diagrams and Alan Young the maps. The excursion leaflets and tickets are from David Beeken and Peter Sunderland. We were looked after at Grimsby and Immingham by Garry Crossland of Associated British Ports, by Willie Weir of English Welsh & Scottish Railway and by Toby Thompson of DFDS Tor Line.

We were in danger of neglecting the more westerly end of the line until requests in the press drew offers of help and information from Messrs Crosby, Wilkinson, Goodman and Needham. We hope that they and all the other contributors will be happy with the result.

Your two authors sporting suitable protective headgear during a visit to Grimsby Docks. *(Garry Crossland)*

Contents

The book is not just a history but also a survey of the present day railway scene. The Railways of North Lincolnshire are still very much in business, as are the Ports, which they created. Our choice of front cover photo was to emphasise the importance of the modern day operation. Thanks to Dave Enefer for taking it specially. And to balance, the rear cover is a reminder that the story includes some esoteric features, once much enjoyed by connoisseurs.

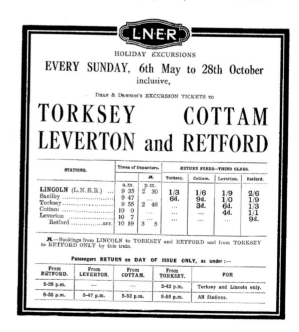

2

Trans Pennine to the Seaside

A Manchester to Hull train passing Hatfield Main Colliery, east of Stainforth & Hatfield, on 1 May 1981. The four coach unit is a hybrid Trans Pennine and Swindon Cross Country – see inside back cover.

(G W Morrison)

Doncaster has always been a railway town. Once it was famous for the "Plant", the Great Northern loco works, which run parallel to the station on the west side. Some readers will remember when you could see gleaming, freshly out shopped steam locomotives. Today, there is still the odd diesel or electric loco parked between the station and the "Plant", more powerful and faster than their steam forebears, yet for some, less aesthetic.

Out on the main line, the trains are faster and more frequent than could ever have been dreamed in the days of steam. With London trains stopping at Doncaster at least twice an hour, and with most journeys completed in well under two hours, the town generates sizeable traffic in long distance commuting.

Today, the majority of expresses are powered through Doncaster by class 91 electrics in push-pull mode. There are "Eurostars" on some Leeds - London workings and still a handful of diesel High Speed Trains, with a class 43 on each end, which have so revolutionised Inter City travel since the 1970s. More "up to date" but less well liked are the Virgin Voyagers running hourly between Bristol and Newcastle. The main complaint against them is that they are only four coach Diesel Multiple Units, with inadequate luggage space.

A four coach unit would be a luxury indeed on the service we are joining. The usual formation for a "Trans Pennine Express" is a two coach class 158. The service is hourly, through from Manchester Airport to Cleethorpes.

We leave from platform 4, the inside face of the large down island. Immediately north of the station, at Marshgate Junction, the main line splits into three with routes for Leeds, York and Hull/Cleethorpes. We take the right hand option and are very soon joined, at Bentley Junction, by the Doncaster Avoiding Line. This was built in connection with the Immingham project. It joins our route by a flying junction.

Another goods line trails in at Kirk Sandall Junction, whence we are on four tracks. The middle pair are the passenger lines, which serve the island platform at Kirk Sandall Station, built in 1991 at the expense of the South Yorkshire PTE. A little further on, the remains of an earlier station can be glimpsed on the left at Barnby Dun, closed in 1967. At Stainforth Junction, the West Riding & Grimsby Joint Line trails in. This used to carry a limited passenger service through from Leeds to Cleethorpes. For long enough the next station was called Stainforth & Hatfield but in 1990 the name was reversed to appease a local politician. The station has a Network Rail group standard footbridge, an enormous contraption with different gradients to suit various standard requirements and a price tag to ensure that many places have no footbridge at all or even no station at all.

Prestige power at Doncaster. Class A4 No 60008 "Dwight D Eisenhower" accelerating through the station with a non stop up express on 30 March 1962. *(John Oxley)*

Kirk Sandall, seen towards Doncaster in 1997, was part of the PTE expansion programme, which has ground to a halt in the post privatisation morass of political dogma, bureaucracy and uncontrolled cost inflation. *(Stuart Baker)*

Thorne South in 1962. There is also a Thorne North Station at the other end of the town, on the Hull line. *(Alan Young collection)*

WD class 2 – 8 – 0 No 90382 passing Mauds Bridge on 6 April 1964. The sidings in the foreground mark the original canal side route to Doncaster. The train is just entering the 1866 alignment. *(David Holmes)*

At Thorne Junction, the Hull line branches off. Our route continues as quadruple track for a short distance but reduces to double before Thorne South Station, a spartan affair with just an austere shelter on each otherwise bare platform.

At Mauds Bridge, the line comes alongside the Keadby Canal, which it follows closely for the next eight miles. The South Yorkshire Railway, which built this stretch, was also the Canal Company. At Crowle the main station building, long disused, is on the south side of the canal. Access to the platforms was by a swing bridge, removed after the high level road bridge opened in 1972. The full name of the station was Crowle Central. The suffix was derived from the Great Central Railway, not from any proximity to the town, which is nearly two miles away. It was better served by the Axholme Joint Railway whose remains are marked, half a mile further on, by an abutment on the far side of the canal, which itself narrows to accommodate the base of the much larger swing bridge, which carried the railway across.

The original aim of the Railway, like that of the canal, was to reach the Trent. It was only when iron ore was discovered around Scunthorpe that the line was deviated southward in order to cross the Trent. At Keadby Canal Junction, we curve sharply to the right, crossing the canal at 45 degrees on a sliding bridge. This was built in 1925 to replace an earlier swing bridge. Thanks to the angle of the Railway, it is possible for a short stretch of track to move sideways into the canal bank. The bridge is battery powered, though the batteries are recharged from the mains. The operation is controlled by Keadby Canal Junction signal box, which sits at a strange angle to the Railway because it is aligned with the canal. Like the bridge itself, the box is a 1925 replacement, now serving only as a bridge control box as the line is power signalled from Scunthorpe.

Althorpe Station leads direct onto the Keadby Lifting Bridge, an imposing structure with massive rollers and counter weights at the Scunthorpe end. It carries a road alongside the double track railway. It hasn't actually moved since 1960, when the right of navigation was abolished for ships too tall for the fixed bridge. In practice, they had disappeared already.

Once over the bridge, immediately to the right we can see the former Station Master's house at Gunness & Burrington. The station here was on the pre 1916 alignment off the swing bridge. It was not replaced because the lifting bridge made it possible to walk to Althorpe Station. The two mile 1 in 93 Gunness Bank makes little impression on our class 158 but it was a different story in steam days when heavy mineral trains required assistance in the rear. The climb takes us over Scotter Road or Frodingham Viaduct. This used to number no fewer than 85 arches, each of 30ft span. It was built entirely of brick but was filled in for part of its length in 1910-12 to make an embankment. Material for this was dug from Frodingham Cutting, near the top of the 1 in 93, where the Railway bought additional land on the north side, just for this purpose.

Scunthorpe Station is the third to serve the town, which has undergone a gradual name transition. It was opened on 11 March 1928, as part of a scheme to expand goods facilities which swept away the previous station, ½ mile further on. Part of that scheme was the New Yard, which we now see derelict to the right. It had two reception and 22 sorting sidings but closed in May 1990. Another feature of the 1928 scheme was the concrete viaduct, which carries Brigg Road over the Railway near the far end of the New Yard. This replaced a level crossing. The original Frodingham Station, of 1866 with staggered platforms, was located at the far (east) side of Brigg Road. The second Frodingham & Scunthorpe of 1887 was on the near (west) side of the level crossing. The third, 1928 structure began life as Scunthorpe & Frodingham but the suffix was dropped in the late 1960s. The Borough of Scunthorpe was incorporated in 1936, bringing together five villages of which Scunthorpe had been one and Frodingham another.

To make matters even more complicated, there was between 1906 and 1925, a small station called Scunthorpe on the North Lindsey Light Railway. This is the line we see trailing in at Trent Junction, just beyond Brigg Road. A west to north curve was provided as part of the 1928 alterations. This passed under the Brigg Road viaduct but was removed about 1988 when the end arch was filled in. Frodingham Engine Shed, built in 1932, was alongside the surviving north to east side of the triangle between Dawes Lane and Trent Junction. It closed in 1997.

To our right is the massive Corus steel complex, whose internal rail system totals over 90 miles of track. The connection off the main line is at North Lincoln Junction, opposite the coal terminal. The line trailing in at Foreign Ore Branch Junction is not connected to the internal system but is a main line branch used for delivering full trainloads of iron ore.

The whole environment is a sort of rusty brown colour until, suddenly, we are back in pastoral green. At Appleby, the railway crosses Ermine Street, the Roman road linking London and the Humber. At this point it is now the B1207. Since 2003, the level crossing has been operated from a portakabin whilst they decide whether or not to reuse the 1885 signal box. The up platform and main station building were immediately beyond the crossing. The down platform was staggered eastward.

The situation is the same at Elsham where, until 2003, traditional level crossing gates were protected by semaphores and operated from a wheel in the 1885 signal box. Now there are lifting barriers protected by colour lights worked from a portakabin. The up platform and station building were on the west side of the crossing with the down platform

Dating from 1886, Medge Hall box gained a mains water supply in 2004. *(John Holroyd)*

staggered back towards Appleby.

We now curve in towards Wrawby Junction and the start of the Barnetby layout, which has become something of a mecca for aficionados of semaphore signalling and diesel haulage. Guest houses do a trade in people coming to watch and photograph the freight traffic passing Barnetby on its way into and out of Immingham. There can be up to a dozen trains passing each hour. There are other locations, which can beat this number with multiple unit passenger trains, but here the majority traffic comprises heavy freight.

Not that the layout is at anything like its maximum extent. Barnetby West box went in 1970 and the sidings are largely disused. The three way junction at Wrawby is controlled from the 137 lever box commissioned in 1916. Still with the original Mckenzie & Holland frame, it was refurbished and re-windowed in 2000. Barnetby East is a more modest 72 lever box, dating from 1914 when the route to Brocklesby was widened to four tracks. It too retains the original Mckenzie & Holland frame and has recently been refurbished with new windows.

In between the two boxes is Barnetby Station, with its Network Rail group standard footbridge giving access to the two island platforms. It has been unstaffed since withdrawal of the through London trains in 1993.

Quadruple track between Barnetby and Brocklesby was reduced back to double in the 1980s. Then, in 1995, the down (westbound) goods line was reinstated so there are now three tracks. There is less need for an up goods line because most eastbound

Passing Godnow Bridge on 6 July 1975. The station, which only ever had a market day service, last appeared in the timetable in February 1917.
(Alan Young)

A train of empty hopper wagons passing Althorpe Station and Keadby Bridge on 31 August 1965.
(Geoffrey Lewthwaite)

Scunthorpe & Frodingham, about 1960 with class 04 No 63696 waiting between duties as Gunhouse banker. The extensive New Yard was built at the same time as the station in the late 1920s. It is now derelict. *(John Oxley)*

Looking east from the viaduct which carries Brigg Road, about 1960. The building on the right is the second Frodingham & Scunthorpe Station (1887 – 1928).
(John Oxley)

Elsham looking east in 1973. The signal box has come back into use, early in 2005, after two years in a portakabin.
(Alan Young)

The main building at Barnetby in July 1974. It has been out of railway use since destaffing in 1993. Originally the building fronted direct onto the up platform but the latter became an island when track was quadrupled in 1914.
(Alan Young)

trains are empty, giving faster acceleration. Also, once clear of Brocklesby, they will be out of the way of passenger traffic.

The ornate building at Brocklesby dates from opening in 1848, and is a measure not of the station's importance for traffic but of its proximity to the seat of the Earl of Yarborough, the original Company chairman. The station closed in 1993. It was 1½ miles from Brocklesby Village, which is actually closer to Habrough Station. The signal box sits on the eastbound platform. Chris' father worked this box for a time, getting there from Grimsby on his bicycle, assisted where possible by lifts on goods trains. Mrs Bates insisted on living in town rather than country, so Dad eventually got moved to Friargate box.

Nearly all freight traffic now branches off towards Immingham. Passenger trains take the gentle right hand curve. The third side of the triangle, now just a single track, trails in before Habrough Station. This became unstaffed when "paytrains" were introduced in June 1969. Evidently, this was thought unbecoming a station with through London trains, so staff were reintroduced in August 1970. At that time, Habrough was the nearest railhead for the Tor Line passenger ships from Immingham to Gothenburg and Amsterdam but they ceased in 1977. Eventually, in 1993, Habrough lost the London trains with their slam door stock and the opportunity was taken to withdraw staff from here, as well as from Barnetby and Market Rasen.

To the left, the skyline is dominated by the industries along the Humber Bank and by some of the pollution which it propels into the atmosphere. An 1883 MS&L box survives at Roxton Sidings with original 18 lever frame. There then follow three village stations served only by trains from Barton on Humber. Stallingborough, Healing and Great Coates have all been unstaffed since June 1969. At all three, the main buildings survive out of railway use. There used to be a train starting from Great Coates for the biscuit factory workers. It ran all stations to Cleethorpes at 5.20pm Mondays to Thursdays and 4.20 on Fridays. In March 1961, the Friday departure was brought forward to 2.28pm, presumably to reflect a reduction in working hours at the factory. The loco came light from Immingham, picking up the empty carriages at Ulceby. It was the return working of one of the early morning "unadvertised workmen" which ran from Cleethorpes to Immingham stopping at Great Coates.

At Marsh Junction, the 44 lever signal box stands in the middle of the triangle formed by the Great Coates branch. The east curve was removed in 1990. Great Coates is a strange name for the branch because we have already passed through Great Coates Station on the main line. The branch is the connection both to the west side of Grimsby Docks, the only part still rail served, and to the Grimsby District Light Railway, the goods line to Immingham alongside which the electric tramway used to run. There were very occasional instances of passenger trains being diverted via the Grimsby District Light

The Cleethorpes bound platform at Stallingborough in 1973. Since demolished, the building was the subordinate up side structure. The main building is on the down side, out of railway use. *(Alan Young)*

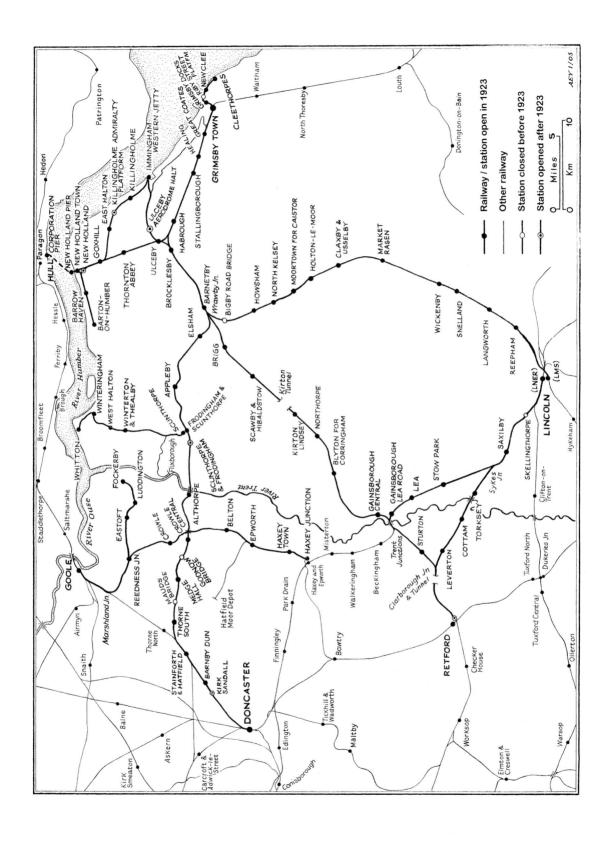

Class 114 Nos 54018/53047 passing Friargate Crossing on 4 May 1987. Between here and the next box, Littlefield Lane, there used to be a loop on the up side, where engines would wait. When Chris` father worked Friargate Box, loco crews would come up for a brew. *(G W Morrison)*

Railway in the event of engineering work on the main line between Brocklesby and Grimsby Town. Stuart Baker once travelled that way behind a Deltic working a Kings Cross - Cleethorpes.

Grimsby Town Station is well maintained. The overall roof was renewed in 1978. Besides the three existing platforms, there used to be a bay at the Cleethorpes end of platform 1 but this is now a car park. Outside is the Yarborough Hotel, now a pub, which was built in 1851 and named after the Chairman of the Railway. A landmark seen on departing Grimsby is the very tall Garden Street signal box. Disused since 1993, the wooden structure sits on top of a large brick base. This was the junction for the East Lincolnshire Line, closed to passengers in 1970. The level crossing is now controlled by cctv from the next box at Pasture Street. This is a flat roof structure, built in 1962 to replace both the previous Pasture Street and Holmes Street which was only a few yards further on. It was Holmes Street which had previously signalled the south to east curve coming in from the East Lincolnshire line. Pasture Street gained a panel in 1985 to control the entire route to Cleethorpes, when the track was singled. In 1993, the panel was extended to take in the Grimsby Town area. There is a passing loop at Pasture Street. Apart from this, there is just the single track making its way through

what was once an extensive layout. To the right was Grimsby Loco Shed and the wagon repair shops. To the left was Marsh Street Goods Yard.

Before the First World War, Grimsby Docks was the station for Continental passengers. Now it is just a short single platform, served only by the Barton trains. Straight ahead is the Dock Office, still used by Associated British Ports and very well appointed inside. In front of this is the Cleethorpe Road flyover, built in 1967 to replace the level crossing which spanned the diverging lines, right to Cleethorpes and left into the Western Docks.

Curving sharply to the right, we follow the one remaining track past the side of the Dock Office, where there was a further junction for the Eastern and Fish Docks. The workmen's halt at Riby Street was just beyond the level crossing at Fish Dock Road. The fish docks themselves are now part derelict and part used as a marina.

New Clee used to receive football specials for the Grimsby Town ground at Blundell Park. Today the station is almost derelict, a request stop served only by the Barton trains and only in daylight. To avoid complicated seasonal footnotes, the first train stops at 8.46 am and the last at 3.03pm all year round. Except on Sundays when all trains stop by request, giving New Clee a departure as late as 7.56pm but the Sunday service only runs from May to

Grimsby Town in Autumn 1975, before the roof was renewed. *(Mike Allen)*

With work on the roof in progress, a class 105 DMU calls at Grimsby Town on 2 July 1978. When first introduced, these Cravens units worked through from Cleethorpes to London in six car formation.
(Alan Young)

September. Does the station do any business whatsoever? Immediately beyond New Clee, on the left hand side, was an expanse of fish van sidings, which on Sundays could be filled by excursion trains having worked into Cleethorpes.

Approaching the terminus, today's single track opens out to provide a fairly extensive layout. When it was remodelled in 1985, it still had to allow for through London trains, so there are still some carriage sidings and there is still access into five of the six platforms. There is no track in platform 4 but platforms 5 and 6 are still signalled, even if the rails are buried under sand dunes. The original station building, now a pub, stands half way along platform 1. We can see how, in 1885, they extended the railway by moving the focal point of the station to the wooden building, beyond the buffer stops. We exit the station this way, passing the clock tower, its one distinguishing feature.

So this is it. The resort developed by the Great Central Railway, more than a century ago. It is difficult now to appreciate what a breath of fresh air this would have been to those more used to the coal mines and steel works of South Yorkshire. We take a bracing walk towards the Kingsway terminus of the Cleethorpes Coast Light Railway, not operating in November. Out to sea, we observe the forts built during the First World War to stop the enemy from sailing up the Humber. There are a handful of ships at anchor, maybe waiting for the tide. One of the latest 32,400 ton DFDS Tor Line vessels is steaming out towards Spurn Head and the open sea.

Fish Dock Road crossing and signal box in July 1978.
(Alan Young)

Driving trailer 56044 leading a class 114 set at Cleethorpes on 28 July 1979. There is no longer any track in platform 4 but the clock tower still surmounts the station building. *(Tom Heavyside)*

.... and Back Again

The tragedy of the fragmented privatised railway is that increased Government investment has just been flushed away in a sea of political dogma, bureaucracy and uncontrolled cost inflation. The result is the near impossibility of achieving service improvements, still worse any kind of network extension.

At the same time, there have emerged one or two sacred cows, services which, however useless, cannot be withdrawn, lest they start a closure controversy, something the Government appears not to want. One such is the Saturdays only service of three trains each way between Cleethorpes and Sheffield by the original MS&L main line. Since 1993, these trains have constituted the only traffic between Wrawby Junction (Barnetby) and Trent Junctions (Gainsborough). The line is closed Sunday to Friday.

The route was a victim of the improving service via Scunthorpe and, by the late 1960s, only three or four trains a day continued to run via Gainsborough. In the late 1980s, BR made a formal closure application. This sparked a response, which threatened to assume similar proportions to the Settle & Carlisle issue. The latter had been the subject of an eight year campaign, culminating in the Government's 1989 decision to keep it open. Many BR managers were left feeling that there was no point in following Government instructions to initiate closures. The result would be just eight years of wasted effort.

In 1991, the Gainsborough closure was called off. Then, two years later, the service was reduced to Saturdays only and nobody said a word.

We join DMU No 144012 on the 2.56pm Cleethorpes to Sheffield. The first hurdle to overcome is the conductor who tries, quite reasonably, to persuade us that this is not the

Preserved steam at Brigg. B1 No 61264 calls with the "Lincolnshire Poacher" railtour on 25 October 2003.
(Dave Enefer)

Brigg signal box with manual level crossing gates. The box dates from 1885 though it gained a new 30 lever frame in 1923. *(F W Smith)*

express to Sheffield. There are a few local passengers to Habrough and Barnetby, after which just a dozen remain. A mile beyond Wrawby Junction, the track singles, but it doubles again on the approach to Brigg where a relief signalman operates conventional level crossing gates from a wheel in the box. Two passengers alight. The train stands for a good five minutes before continuing, its payload now down to about ten.

Approaching Scawby & Hibaldstow, it looks as though the station car park is full but its an optical illusion. The former goods yard is just full of scrap.

The double track ends at Kirton Lime Sidings where the MS&L provided a very tall signal box, enabling the signalman to see over the road bridge. The original 15 lever frame is still in use, from 1886. The Lime Sidings are still connected but overgrown. They haven't been used since 1992.

We pass through the 1,334 yard Kirton Tunnel before coming to a stand in Kirton Lindsey Station. There are no customers but we are again obliged to wait more than five minutes before departure time. Time to admire the well preserved station building.

It cannot be often that Northorpe passing loop is required by traffic but it remains serviceable, controlled from the original 1886 box with its 17 lever frame. Into early BR days, Northorpe still offered a full range of services: Passenger, parcels, livestock, horse box, carriage - that means you could have a private carriage conveyed on a wagon attached to a passenger train. You could also park a motor vehicle at the station, from which you could send a telegram. If you needed to telephone about

any of these matters, the number was "Northorpe 1". Unfortunately, business was insufficient to sustain the station beyond 1955.

It is hard to imagine that Gainsborough Central was once a major station with imposing façade and overall roof. Again, there is a six minute interval in which to survey the scene. One passenger alights with a bicycle. A few years ago, the then train operator Northern Spirit removed the waiting shelter from the up platform for use elsewhere. This invoked the wrath of the Rail Regulator who found no justification in the Company's defence of "no passengers". So Northern Spirit relented and provided a replacement, conceding that if someone did miss the 15.00 to Cleethorpes and did elect to wait for the next train, six days and seven nights would indeed be a long time without shelter.

We're back on double track for the short run to Gainsborough Trent Junctions, where the 1964 signal box controls the layout on both sides of the River. Originally this was impossible and separate boxes had to be provided at the two junctions. Still known as the Joint Line, the former Great Northern and Great Eastern route converges on the left from Lincoln, shares our double track over the viaduct, then immediately diverges in the direction of Doncaster. Lincoln to Sheffield trains come via Trent Junctions, so we are now back on the seven day week railway.

West Burton power station, commissioned in 1966, was the first to receive coal on the "merry go round" principle by which the hopper wagons are loaded at the colliery and discharged at the

By 1989, Kirton Lindsey had been reduced to a single platform, a simple shelter replacing the large building which is out of railway use.   *(Alan Young)*

Gainsborough Central
entrance portico about 1970.
(Dave Enefer collection)

The station originally had an
overall roof. Looking towards
Retford about 1900.
(Dave Enefer collection)

From an almost identical
vantage point, Gainsborough
Central in 2004.
(Martin Bairstow)

Great Central "Large Director" class D11 No 62664 "Princess Mary" calls at Gainsborough Central with a train from Cleethorpes to Sheffield in 1950.

(Paul Needham)

destination, whilst the train continues to move slowly. The operation continues today with coal imported through Immingham. Because the direct route is closed six days a week, this traffic has to be worked via Scunthorpe and Doncaster. The extra cost includes the need to employ twice as many drivers.

A well used double track trails in at Clarborough Junction. This was the original main line from Lincoln, closed in 1959 but subsequently reopened as far as the coal fired power station at Cottam, whose cooling towers can be seen on the horizon.

It was the impending development of West Burton and Cottam, which forced changes to the layout at Retford, commissioned on 14 June 1965. The anticipated additional coal traffic could not have been accommodated over the flat crossing with the East Coast Main Line. After passing Thrumpton Signal Box, our train drops down at 1 in 100 into the low level platforms, where four of our remaining passengers alight. If these people want main line connections, they will have to follow a short footpath leading up to the platforms in the former Great Northern Station. As soon as our train restarts for Sheffield, it will pass under the Main Line and then climb until it meets, at Whisker Hill, the loop from the Main Line station, which will join by a flying junction. Before 1965, freight and non stop passenger trains would have gone straight across the Main Line on the level. Our train would have curved sharply to the right to gain the Main Line Station, from which it would have curved round to Whisker Hill, then only a flat junction.

58032 leaving West Burton power station with an empty "merry go round" on 27 March 1990.

(G W Morrison)

31271 pulls away from Retford with a Saturdays only Chesterfield to Skegness train on 28 July 1979. Dating from 1889, Thrumpton box was converted from a lever frame to a panel in 1965. It was comprehensively refurbished during early 2005 *(G W Morrison)*

Class J11 No 64354 negotiates the north to east curve at Retford, which was removed as part of the 1965 alterations. *(Paul Needham collection)*

The Manchester, Sheffield & Lincolnshire Railway

This work in future ages, when we shall long have quitted this scene and when perhaps our names will be forgotten, will I hope become a new centre of life with the vast and ever increasing commerce of the World and a most important link in the connection of the East and West.   Prince Albert - 18 April 1849

The subject of this book is, very largely, the eastern section of the Manchester, Sheffield & Lincolnshire Railway, formed on 27 July 1846 by the amalgamation of four Companies:

The Sheffield, Ashton Under Lyne & Manchester Railway

The Sheffield & Lincolnshire Junction Railway

The Great Grimsby & Sheffield Junction Railway

The Grimsby Docks Company

The SA&MR was the main line between Sheffield and Manchester, which had been completed on 22 December 1845. Centrepiece was the 3 mile 22 yard Woodhead Tunnel, at the time the longest railway tunnel in the world.

The S&LJR was an embryonic concern, hoping to build a line from Sheffield to Gainsborough with a branch to Lincoln. It was authorised on 3 August 1846, a week after the amalgamation. Its Act might have come a year earlier had it not been for the congestion in Parliament caused by the "Railway Mania", which was then at its peak. The planned last seven miles into Lincoln ran very close to the route sought by the Great Northern Railway for its Gainsborough to Lincoln line. The Act determined that the Great Northern should build this section over which the MS&LR would exercise running powers from Sykes Junction.

The Great Grimsby & Sheffield Junction had been authorised on 30 June 1845. Its projected main line extended from Gainsborough both to Grimsby and to New Holland, for the Hull ferry. It included a branch from Barnetby to Market Rasen. Powers for this were extended to Lincoln under a second Act of 26 June 1846, which also authorised the Barton branch and the operation of steamships across the Humber.

Anticipating amalgamation, the three Companies acted in close cooperation from the Autumn of 1845. They hoped to add to their combine, the East Lincolnshire Railway, then newly authorised between Grimsby and Louth, but that fell into the hands of the Great Northern Railway. They were more successful in extending their influence over the Grimsby Docks Company.

Incorporated on 8 August 1845, the Docks Company was a successor to the Grimsby Haven Company, created by Act of Parliament in 1796. This Company had diverted the River Freshney so as to provide a constant flow of water into what became known as the Old Dock, opened in 1801. The purpose of the new Docks Company was to create a larger rail served port centred upon what was to become the Royal Dock.

The "Railway Mania", of the mid 1840s, was a period of massive railway enactment. The years that followed saw many authorised schemes falter for lack of capital. The Manchester, Sheffield & Lincolnshire did very well to carry out its original purpose within a commendable timescale.

The first line is opened

The first section to open, on 1 March 1848, was from Grimsby to New Holland. The East Lincolnshire Railway, from Grimsby to Louth, opened the same day. That enterprise had been leased to the Great Northern Railway but they still made a joint announcement, advertising through services from Louth to New Holland and thence by Railway owned ferry to Hull. As explained in the New Holland chapter, this co-operation did not last long

Completion of the Main Line

Exactly eight months after the first opening, on 1 November 1848, the operational line was extended both to Brigg and to Market Rasen. The latter was a terminus for only seven weeks until opening through to Lincoln on 18 December. The Main Line was

Scawby & Hibaldstow looking towards Brigg in October 1965. It closed in February 1968. *(Geoffrey Lewthwaite)*

The main building at Brocklesby in 1986. It was always disproportionate to the likely traffic but the Earl of Yarborough lived nearby.

(Alan Young)

Class O2 No 63976 approaching Sturton with coal empties from Immingham on 31 March 1961.

(John Oxley)

extended to Gainsborough on 2 April 1849. There was then a short wait of only 15 weeks for the remaining gap to be filled, from Gainsborough through Retford to Woodhouse Junction, 5½ miles east of Sheffield.

Opening this stretch, on 16 July 1849, completed the main line of the Manchester, Sheffield & Lincolnshire Railway, right through from Manchester to Grimsby and to New Holland (for Hull). The first passenger timetable offered five trains each way between Sheffield and either Grimsby or New Holland. It is not clear from the advertisement whether any of the trains divided at Brocklesby or whether Grimsby passengers had to change. It is clear that the principal destination was Hull. In some cases, journey time to Grimsby was slightly longer than to Hull, despite the ferry crossing.

The third class fare from Manchester to Hull was 9s 3d, exactly the 1d per mile allowed under Gladstone's 1844 Act. This required at least one train a day in each direction, Sundays, Good Friday and Christmas Day excepted, to convey third class carriages, fitted with seats and a roof, stopping at every station and averaging at least 12 miles per hour. This was the "Parliamentary train", generally the first of the day. From the outset, the MS&L exceeded the minimum requirement by offering two "Parliamentary" trains on this route. The 6.15am and 8.00 from Sheffield were the "Parliamentaries". The 12.14, 4.05 and 5.36pm were first and second class only. On slow trains, second class cost more than 1½

times and first class exactly double the third class fare. There was a further premium for the "Express".

New Holland to Hull counted as 3 miles for charging purposes. In British Railways days, the working timetable had it as a rather exact 2 miles 32 chains. The truth must have depended on the tide. It was 66 miles from Sheffield to New Holland. Journey time was around 2 hours 50 minutes on a "Parliamentary" and 2 hours 25 minutes by "Express". That was in the first month of operation. More than a century and a half later, the similar distance between Sheffield and Grimsby Town takes 1 hour 30 to 35 minutes on a "Trans Pennine Express" and 2 hours on the Saturday train via Brigg.

Grimsby Docks

Work started in 1846 on what became known as the Royal Dock. A total of 138 acres of land were reclaimed from the Humber, the whole area around the Dock being beyond the previous high water mark. The Dock itself covered 20 acres. Access from the sea was by two locks, one of 300ft by 70ft, the other 200ft by 45ft. Hydraulic power for the gates came from the 300ft high brick tower, which was to become the dominant Grimsby landmark. Outside the locks was a tidal basin, partly enclosed by wooden piers. The Royal Dock opened on 27 May 1852.

The railway beyond Grimsby Town to the docks must have been in use as a contractors line from

Grimsby Royal Dock, June 1959.

(John Oxley)

1848. It was certainly used on 18 April 1849 when Prince Albert came to lay the foundation stone of the new dock. It opened to passenger traffic on 1 August 1853 with stations at Grimsby Docks and Grimsby Pier. The former is still in use but the Pier Station, near the Dock Tower, was converted during the 1870s to serve as a hostel for migrants from the Continent who might take refuge there before contemplating the onward journey to the New World. In later years, steamer passengers either used Grimsby Docks Station or were conveyed in through carriages direct to the quayside.

Work began in 1873 on a connection, known as the Union Dock, between the Royal and the Old Dock of 1801. At the same time, a new 26 acre dock was built at right angles to the Old Dock. The combined enterprise was named the Alexandra Dock in deference to the Princess of Wales who attended the opening of the first stage on 22 July 1879. The entire facility was in operation from Summer 1880. The Alexandra Dock has two arms. The westerly one, now used by car carriers, is the 26 acre dock opened in 1880. The southern arm, now hardly used, is the original 1801 dock which is traversed by the Corporation Bridge and which is now home to the "Lincoln Castle" serving as a pub.

Rail access to the Alexandra Dock was provided by the 2 mile Great Coates branch, opened on 27 March 1879. This line was rebuilt on a more north westerly alignment in connection with the Immingham project. The old route was abandoned after the new one opened on 4 January 1909. Part of it is now Boulevard Avenue. The tracks at Alexandra Dock continued on to the west side of the Royal Dock, where they met the line which had come in from Grimsby Docks Station and which crossed the Union Dock by a swing bridge.

To shunt the docks, the MS&L bought six Manning Wardle 0 - 6 - 0 saddle tanks from Logan & Hemingway, the contractors who had used them for building the Alexandra Dock. They also purchased five 0 - 4 - 0 saddle tanks new from Manning Wardle. Two of these survived long enough to be classified Y2 by the LNER.

A class which shunted Grimsby Docks for nearly 50 years was the J63 0 - 6 - 0, of which seven were built between 1906 and 1914. They were based at the six road engine shed, just south of Grimsby Docks Station. This lost much of its main line work after Immingham Shed opened in 1912. By the 1930s, half the shed had been demolished. It continued as a sub shed of Immingham until 1957. Another prominent class of shunter was the J50 with its distinctive sloping side tanks, designed to give the driver a better view. By 1935, 15 of these were allocated to Immingham and its sub sheds at Grimsby and New Holland. They were displaced after the Second World War by the J94 "Austerity" saddle tanks, of which the LNER bought 75 from the War Department. 25 of these were allocated to

Standard 4 – 6 – 0 No 75056 passing Grimsby Docks with the afternoon fish for Nottingham on 27 March 1961. A Cravens DMU, later class 105, waits for the signal to restart for Cleethorpes. (Roger Hockney)

"Black Five" 4 – 6 – 0 No 45217 passing Cleethorpe Road Junction and the Grimsby Dock Office with an excursion for Cleethorpes on 27 August 1961. *(Roger Hockney*

Immingham, including 68077 which is preserved on the Keighley & Worth Valley Railway. They, in turn, gave way to diesel shunters, the first of which arrived in 1954.

Grimsby Docks remained in railway ownership until nationalisation in 1948, when they became a part of the all embracing British Transport Commission. On the break up of the Commission in 1963, the state owned ports were divided between the British Railways Board and the British Transport Docks Board, the former generally taking those with BR passenger ferries. Grimsby went to the Docks Board, which was privatised in 1983 becoming Associated British Ports.

In 1976, BR announced closure of the rail link into Grimsby Docks, blaming a 90% loss of traffic in just four years. The decision was reversed in 1978 following a revival in steel traffic. By this time, access was only via the Great Coates Branch. There were no tracks going in to the docks at Cleethorpe Road Junction, near Grimsby Docks Station. The connection between east and west sides, over Union Dock swing bridge was severed in 1968. The Union Dock itself was widened so as to admit car carrier ships into Alexandra Dock where a roll on - roll off berth was provided for the import of Volks Wagen products. Beginning in 1975, this trade has developed into the largest activity in the Port of Grimsby. Rail traffic now is minimal.

L. N. E. R. FURLOUGH
For conditions see back
Available for three days including day of issue
Grimsby Town
GRIMSBY TOWN to
LEEDS (CENTRAL)
LEEDS C
Via Hemsworth
3rd. Class

2272

L. N. E. R. FURLOUGH
For conditions see back
Available for three days including day of issue
Grimsby Town
LEEDS C
3rd. Class

2272

British Railways Board (E)
PARKING TICKET FOR MOTOR CAR OR THREE-WHEELED VEHICLE AT
NEW HOLLAND (TOWN)
Registration No.......................
Fee 1/0
Available on day of issue only
For conditions see over

0604

0604

L. C. L. R.
THIS TICKET is issued subject to the regulations and notices of the Company
HUMBERSTON (Beach)
TO
HUMBERSTON (North Sea Lane)
AVAILABLE ON DAY OF ISSUE ONLY
L119—Williamson, Printer Ashton

3489

Approaching the west end of Kirton Tunnel (1,325 yards) on 23 May 1961   *(John Marshall)*

One of the Railway`s objectives, upon reaching Grimsby, was to establish steamship services to the Continent. The sister ships, "Northenden" and "Warrington" were built for the MS&L in 1886. This model is displayed in the Grimsby Dock Office.   *(Chris Bates)*

The Dock Office is well appointed inside and still used by Associated British Ports for its original purpose. Garry Crossland, who assisted us with the book, is employed at Grimsby. Besides his regular job, he is responsible for the archives, for which purpose he has converted an old police cell in the basement. The mural gives the place a much better outlook.   *(Chris Bates)*

Cleethorpes

62665 "Mons" pulls away from Cleethorpes on 25 May 1958. 61296 waits its turn in the carriage sidings.
(Martin Bairstow collection)

A branch to Cleethorpes had been amongst the earliest ambitions of the Great Grimsby & Sheffield Junction Railway. It had been included in the Company's Bill deposited in November 1845 at the peak of the "Railway Mania" but was dropped, presumably to save other parts of the Bill, which emerged as the GG&SJ Act 1846.

The branch was eventually authorised in 1861 and opened for passenger traffic on 6 April 1863. Widening to double track was completed on 25 May 1874. Development of Cleethorpes as a resort was proceeding slowly. The 1,200 ft pleasure pier had been opened in 1872. Eight years later, the Railway decided to extend the station towards the pier. At that point, the local authority tempted the MS&L with a proposal to build sea defences so as to protect the cliffs to the east of the pier and use the area for re c reational purposes.

The Railway rose to the challenge, obtaining Parliamentary powers in its Acts of 1881 and 1884 to acquire land, buy out the pier company, light the promenade and build swimming baths, tea rooms, a colonnade and even a photographic studio. Some of the attractions commanded an entry fee, administered in the only way the Railway knew, by the issue of Edmondson Card tickets. By the turn of the Century, the Great Central could bring as many as 30,000 excursionists a day into Cleethorpes and

make money out of them over and above anything collected in fares.

If we look at Cleethorpes departures in 1910, we find a lot of variety in the basic year round service but not a great density. The day begins with a true "Parliamentary" at 5.40am, all stations to Retford. Next, at 6.30 is an Express to Sheffield Victoria. In common with all timetabled trains, this stops at New Clee, Grimsby Docks and Grimsby Town, then Brigg, Gainsborough, and Retford where it arrives only nine minutes behind the stopper. The 7.00 is all stations to Lincoln (GN). The 7.45 is another all stations to Retford, except that Great Coates, Healing and Stallingborough are request stops to take up passengers for Barnetby or beyond. The 8.30 is for New Holland Pier stopping, after Grimsby Town, only at Habrough, Ulceby, Goxhill and New Holland Town.

The 8.43am is an express to Leeds Central calling at Frodingham, Crowle, Wakefield Westgate and Holbeck. It stops by request at Habrough to take up for Wakefield and beyond. This train emphasised the Great Central's joint ownership of the West Riding & Grimsby line (Stainforth & Hatfield to Wakefield Westgate) and running powers thence into Leeds. See *The Great Northen Railway in the West Riding*. The train did not run during the 1930s but was revived after 1948 and ran into the DMU era. In the early 1960s, it was the regular preserve of loco No 61406, which came back on the 4.10pm Leeds - Cleethorpes.

The 8.55 from Cleethorpes was all stations to Penistone via Doncaster and Barnsley Court House. It was followed by the 9.50 all stations to Lincoln, which has two complications. Great Coates, Healing and Stallingborough are again by request to take up for Barnetby and beyond. On a Thursday, Brigg market day, there are extra carriages, to be detached at Brocklesby and merged with a train from New Holland. The 10.30 is through to Liverpool Central, a journey of exactly six hours, beginning all stations as far as Retford albeit that Great Coates, Healing, Stallingborough and Habrough are by request to take up only. The 11.20 all stations to New Holland Pier is followed by the 12 noon to Grimsby Town. There is another all stations to Retford at 12.30pm and so the day goes on. Some of the complicated request stops may have been in response to pleas from individual passengers, channelled via the local station master.

The foregoing was not enough to fill all six platforms at Cleethorpes, nor the carriage sidings. Until we come to the Summer extras. Peter Sunderland has kindly loaned an LNER working timetable for excursion trains dated Summer 1935. It shows conditional paths to which many special trains would adhere. There would always be some more for which there was no established working. Besides advertised excursions, there were those arranged for Sunday Schools, Working Mens Clubs and the like. This publication is for the Great Northern Section, not Great Central so our interest is only at the periphery.

There is a day excursion leaving Cleethorpes at 6.55am for London Kings Cross. Return departure is at 12 midnight getting back to Cleethorpes at 3.50am. This is via the East Lincolnshire Line with reversal at Grimsby Town. 11 coaches are required and the guard's job is a Cleethorpes turn. There is an evening excursion at 6.03pm from Cleethorpes to Mablethorpe, arriving back at 11.34pm, again with reversal at Grimsby Town both ways. Seating capacity of 1,000 is required and the guard is again a Cleethorpes man.

There is a half day excursion from Kings Cross to Cleethorpes at 10.10am, arriving at 1.57pm and leaving again at 6.38. This uses the Goods Junction to Holmes Junction curve and calls at Grimsby Docks. A full day excursion leaves Bradford Exchange at 7.15am and Leeds Central at 7.50, the two 5 coach portions amalgamating at Wakefield Westgate. After serving memorable GN West Riding stations such as Laisterdyke, Drighlington & Adwalton and Nostell, the train takes the West Riding & Grimsby Joint to Scunthorpe and Cleethorpes. At least, that is what the printed version said. But the "Company's Servant" to whom this booklet was issued, has inserted a stop at Grimsby Docks in each direction and has then painstakingly added one minute to every station arrival and departure time on the way back, giving an amended Bradford Exchange arrival at 10.56pm.

"Deltic" No 55021 "Argyll & Sutherland Highlander" shunting empty carriages at Cleethorpes on 28 July 1979. *(G W Morrison)*

The Railway bought Cleethorpes Pier in 1884, using Edmondson Card tickets to charge admission to this and other attractions such as the Grimsby Dock Tower.
(Martin Bairstow collection)
(Ticket Garry Crossland collection)

New Clee looking towards Grimsby about 1968. Nominally still open, the station has lost all of its business with the demolition of nearby housing which used to supply custom for the Immingham and Great Coates workmen`s trains.
(Alan Young collection)

One of those workmen`s trains between New Clee and Cleethorpes behind D5801 in 1964.   *(Roger Hockney*

Nine locomotives wait in New Clee sidings with their return excursions on Sunday 28 June 1959. From the left: 61165 for Rotherham Central, 61377 for Doncaster, 61230 for Fitzwilliam, 62668 for Sutton in Ashfield, 61824 for Sheffield Victoria, 61208 and 61231 for Worksop, 61803 for Harworth Colliery and 62660 for Kirkby in Ashfield. *(N E Stead)*

Class B1 No 61049 on the 5.57pm stopper to Doncaster, about a mile out of Cleethorpes. Hot ash in the smokebox has caused paint on the door to blister. *(Roger Hockney)*

Grimsby Fish

"Britannia" Class 4 – 6 – 2 No 70041 "Sir John Moore" passing Cleethorpe Road Junction with fish for Manchester on 24 April 1962. A few "Britannias" were at Immingham Shed in the early 1960s, having been displaced by diesels on passenger work out of London Liverpool Street. *(Roger Hockney)*

In 1852, the year the Royal Dock was completed, some 500 tons of fish were landed at Grimsby. During the next decade, that figure increased to over 10,000 tons, principally through the completion in 1856 of a specialist fish dock immediately to the east of the Royal Dock. To help ensure that fish actually came to the new installation, the MS&LR invested in the Deep Sea Fishing Company, which had a fleet of nine vessels by the end of 1856. Business grew and No 2 Fish Dock was opened in 1877. It was enlarged in 1894 causing the curvature on the Cleethorpes line to be more severe as the original alignment was taken by the new quay. By 1910, the tonnage of fish landed at Grimsby was almost 180,000. Powers for a third dock were obtained in 1912 but the First World War delayed work for nearly 20 years. No 3 Fish Dock, an eastward extension of No 1, was opened in October 1934.

There is a two part article on Grimsby fish traffic in *Trains Illustrated* for May and June 1958. At that time, there were some 300 trawlers based at the port. A trip to the fishing grounds could take from 10 days to three weeks so each day there might be 20 or more vessels landing upward of 800 tons of catch. Rail traffic comprised up to 330 wagons on a Monday, 250 on other weekdays. There were eight dedicated express fish trains plus odd wagons

attached to passenger trains. The latter would involve a shunting engine propelling out of the docks onto the back of a train from Cleethorpes, standing in Grimsby Docks Station. Despite the appearance of large scale activity, danger signs were already p resent. The average load of a van was less than two tons. Some of the large distributors were using road transport for bulk loads, relying on the Railway to c a rry odd boxes to wayside stations plus re t u rning to the Railway with heavy loads in bad weather. The operation re qu i red railway staff to estimate the number of wagons re qu i red in advance of each day. This meant a lot of spare capacity. It also involved a lot of intermediate handling, many of the individual boxes ending up on branch passenger trains. This handling was itself subject to daily fluctuation as loads for diff e rent stations might be amalgamated or given separate vans according to demand.

In May 1964, the National Federation of Fishmongers and Poulterers held their annual conference in Blackpool. They were treated to an address by Mr J P Bearcroft, BR Director of Marketing and Planning. He told them that, over a decade, fish landings had fallen by 22% but rail loadings had gone down by 55%. There were still 25 fish trains running on a typical day, eight from each of Grimsby and Hull, five from Fleetwood and four

Three light engines making their way to the Fish Docks to pick up their loaded trains on 16 April 1964. B1 No 61023 "Hirola" is coupled to 9Fs 92038 and 92184. *(Roger Hockney)*

9F No 92195 taking the Great Northern route at Pasture Street with fish for London on 18 April 1963. *(Roger Hockney)*

from Aberdeen. The eight Grimsby trains were averaging 188 vans, carrying 334 tons of fish. BR wanted to stay in the fish business but required a payload of 150 tons per train to make operation viable. They proposed to reduce the number of trains nationally to nine, of which Grimsby would have three: one to Sheffield and Manchester, one to Lincoln, Peterborough, Hitchin and London and one with vans for various stations as far as Swansea, Plymouth and Southampton, this latter to amalgamate at Hexthorpe, near Doncaster, with the corresponding train from Hull. There would be no onward carriage by train beyond the specified railheads. If the fish wanted to travel further they would have to be transferred onto road.

The reaction of the Industry was to transfer the entire traffic to road haulage. By late 1965, there was only one fish train out of Grimsby conveying a mere 15 vans. Even this finished during 1967. As we saw in *Railways of Blackpool & The Fylde,* the same thing happened at Fleetwood.

Four decades later, it is not just the rail traffic which has gone, but most of the deep sea fishing industry as well. Food processing remains an important part of the Grimsby economy but most of the fish is brought in by road.

Class 9F No 92038 passing Wellowgate box with the 5.13pm fish to Manchester on 17 April 1964.

(Roger Hockney)

70039 "Sir Christopher Wren" negotiating Cleethorpe Road Junction with the 4.30pm fish to Whitland, South Wales, on 24 April 1964.

(Roger Hockney)

Trawlers along the North Wall.
(Peter Sunderland collection)

The coaling berths in Grimsby
Fish Docks.
(Peter Sunderland collection)

Fish traffic just survived into
the diesel era. D6800 (later
37100) passing Cleethorpe
Road Junction on 10 April
1964. *(Roger Hockney)*

New Holland

B1 No 61144 waiting to depart New Holland Pier for Cleethorpes on 23 February 1957. The third coach is a CL (composite lavatory), with separate loos in the centre. The coach was gangwayed within each class but there was no communication between first and second.
(David Holmes)

Before the arrival of the Railway, the only buildings in New Holland were a small ferry house and the Yarborough Arms Hotel. This had been built in 1826 as part of a scheme to promote New Holland as a ferry point for Hull in competition with the established but longer crossing from Barton. Over the next two decades, New Holland did outflank Barton, taking most of the mail and stage coach business.

In 1848, the arrival of the MS&L promised to transform New Holland into a significant railway port. Rows of houses were built for railway and ferry workers in streets named after towns on the MS&L. Many of the railway staff were employed at the four road engine shed, which was provided for the opening of the line on 1 March 1848.

The main line was built 500 yards out into the Humber. A station, later defined as New Holland Town, was provided at the landward end. From here the platforms continued on either side of the double track until they reached a second station called New Holland Pier. A floating landing stage was installed at the Pier Head in December 1849. This was built in Leeds and transported in sections by canal to Goole, where it was assembled, launched and, finally, taken by tugs to New Holland. It was destroyed in a storm on 18 October 1869 and had to be replaced. To the east of the pier, the Railway built a dock of three

acres and a timber pond, in the hope of New Holland becoming a port in its own right. The Yarborough Arms Hotel was bought by the Railway and rebuilt in 1851.

The importance of New Holland was as a gateway to Hull. In the earliest days of the Railway, it was thought that New Holland might actually lie on the main line from London to Hull. At that very early stage, transhipment onto the ferry didn't seem too much of an inconvenience. Hence the Great Northern Railway seeing a trunk route from London to Hull via Peterborough, East Lincolnshire and New Holland. As the network developed, it soon proved better to carry goods and passengers all the way by rail, even at the cost of greater mileage. The Great Northern soon lost interest in New Holland, whilst even the MS&L began to regard it as only a branch line

The initial train service from New Holland comprised five trains a day, through to Louth. Departures were at 8.00 and 11.00am, 1.15, 3.45 and 7.00pm. In each case the ferry left Hull 30 minutes earlier. The first train was the "Parliamentary" conveying three classes of accommodation, stopping at every station and taking 1 hour 20 minutes to Louth. The 11.00 and 3.45 were similar, but first and second class only. The other two were expresses taking 58 minutes with a single stop at

Class 114 "Derby Heavyweight" units at New Holland Pier on 27 June 1959. *(John Oxley)*

Coal was delivered in rail wagons to the middle siding between the platform lines at New Holland Pier. It was then taken down to the paddle steamers in these trucks drawn by a mechanical horse. June 1957.

(Peter Sunderland)

Grimsby, also first and second class only.

The service was operated jointly with the Great Northern, but very soon the two Companies fell out. In 1849, the MS&L joined the "Euston Square Confederacy", an alliance with the London & North Western, Midland and Lancashire & Yorkshire Railways, which sought to carve up traffic between London and the North. Put another way, it was an attempt to strangle the Great Northern.

In July 1851, the MS&L stopped running through to Louth and, from 1 December, insisted on having exclusive use of the line between Grimsby and New Holland. The GN obtained an injunction against the MS&L, enforcing its running powers but never resumed actual working to New Holland. For a time, the GN shipped goods direct to Hull from Grimsby, cutting out the rail journey to New Holland, but it soon decided that the best way to Hull was via Doncaster.

After 1874, even the MS&L was offering an express service to Hull Paragon, which was far quicker for long distance passengers than the New Holland route, which settled down to provide a mainly local function between the two banks of the Humber as well as a modest traffic confined to the south side.

The 1910 timetable shows departures almost every hour from New Holland Pier, either to Brocklesby or Cleethorpes. The 5.34pm Cleethorpes runs non stop to Grimsby Town, which is reached in 59 minutes from the ferry leaving Hull. The corresponding morning train is the 8.30 from Cleethorpes, 8.48 from Grimsby Town, which has patrons landing in Hull at 9.50. This train stops at Habrough, Ulceby and Goxhill.

Some of the above would be worked by locos and crews based at New Holland shed, which stood on the south side of the triangular junction. The shed had a two arch overall roof but each of the four tracks entered through an individual arch. Water was drawn from a reservoir in the middle of the triangle, south of New Holland Town Station.

From 1912, New Holland Shed was eclipsed in importance by the large depot at Immingham. It closed in 1938, though engines continued to be stabled there for a long time afterwards. The roof had gone by 1960, leaving a lone diesel shunter, officially based at Immingham, to stand outside.

Class Y3 Sentinel shunter No 21 at New Holland. 32 of this class were delivered to the LNER between 1927 and 1931. All were withdrawn by 1958. A similar Y1 is preserved on the Middleton Railway, Leeds.
(RCTS)

Class J11 No 5301 at New Holland about 1938.   (RCTS)

With dieselisation of the passenger service in 1956, there were nine departures a day from New Holland Pier to Cleethorpes, plus a solitary working through to Lincoln Central at 2.36pm. There was an extra train to Cleethorpes on a Saturday and a year round Sunday service of seven trains. The line was threatened in the Beeching Report but survived until the opening of the Humber Bridge on 24 June 1981, when both Pier and Town stations closed. The following day, a small halt opened just south of the triangular junction with the Barton line allowing New Holland to be served by the "Humberlink" service described in the next chapter.

Today, the pier is used by New Holland Bulk Services, who retain a Sentinel diesel but rail traffic has been very intermittent, almost non existent. The area around the station is piled high with timber, which all moves by road. The Yarborough Arms is now the offices of Howarth Timber. The two hourly passenger service, usually a single car class 153, merits the retention of two out of New Holland's one time five signal boxes and double track until just north of Ulceby Station. The curve thence to Habrough is single. The one to Brocklesby is double and very busy with traffic out of Immingham.

North of Ulceby, the branch retains many traditional features with gated crossings and semaphore signals. Thornton Abbey station remains open for minimal traffic, its main distinguishing feature being the large nameboards. Years ago, the one on the southbound platform parted company with its support fittings but it rests upright at platform level making sure that travellers know the place which they have reached.

Goxhill is much more substantial as regards both traffic and structure. The platforms were raised and resurfaced in the late 1990s. As the train progresses from here towards New Holland, you can see as far as the King George Dock at Hull, where the 59,925 ton "Pride of Hull" or "Pride of Rotterdam" spend all day at the River Berth. These vessels are so large, they can even be seen from the Dock Office at Grimsby on a clear day.

By 1984, Goxhill was one of the few stations still displaying "totems".
(Alan Young)

Goxhill Station looking south in April 1968.
(Geoffrey Lewthwaite)

New Holland Town looking north. The overall roof was replaced by a canopy on the southbound platform but we don`t know at what date.
(Martin Bairstow collection)

Thornton Abbey looking south in 1968. It became unstaffed the following year. The buildings were subsequently demolished but the large nameboard has survived.
(Geoffrey Lewthwaite)

47222 passing Ulceby with a mgr train of coal for Immingham on 27 July 1979. The box dates from 1910. It gained a panel for working Habrough in 1988.
(Tom Heavyside

The Barton Branch

The 3 mile single track branch to Barton on Humber was authorised by the Great Grimsby & Sheffield Junction Act of July 1846. Opened on 1 March 1849, it joined the New Holland line by a triangular junction, just south of New Holland Town. The passenger service was always to New Holland Pier.

In 1910, there were 14 trains each way on weekdays, fairly evenly spaced leaving New Holland between 6.00am and 10.20pm. There was a later service at 11.40pm on Saturdays, whilst the Sunday service gave just four trains each way. Most trains were shown as having connections from Hull but the waiting time at New Holland varied between 10 and 40 minutes.

Diesel multiple units took over the passenger service on 2 July 1956, but the branch was threatened under the Beeching Report. Twice in the 1960s, closure was refused because of the practical difficulty of providing road transport to meet with the ferry.

Many people thought that the branch would close on completion of the Humber Bridge, which would sweep away the previous justification. However, by the start of the 1980s, the political climate was no longer as keen on railway closures.

The then longest suspension bridge in the World opened on 24 June 1981, from Hessle on the North Bank to Barton. This author provided the commentary for BBC Radio when the Queen officially opened it the following month.

On 25 June 1981, with local authority support, a new train service was introduced, hourly between Cleethorpes and Barton, connecting with a bus over the Bridge to Hull. Some of the trains ran semi fast, calling at Grimsby Docks and Town, Habrough, Goxhill and the new platform at New Holland. The service was marketed as "Humberlink" with through tickets to Hull and beyond.

After four years, the frequency was cut back to nine trains per day (four on Sundays), generally at two hourly intervals, stopping at all stations. That has remained the pattern ever since except that the Sunday service has been reduced to Summer only. Traffic has been erode by an improved road network and a through Grimsby to Hull bus service. A class 153 single railcar is sufficient for most journeys. The bus connection to Hull is still shown in the timetable but through fares are no longer available.

Freight on the branch finished with the loss of the chemical traffic from Albright & Wilsons at Barton on Humber.

A DMU driver gives up the electric token from Barton to the signalman at Oxmarshe Crossing, just south of New Holland Station on 14 May 1987. *(RCTS)*

An attraction of the first generation DMUs was the ability to gain a forward view through the cab. Arriving at Barrow Haven on 27 April 1968. *(Geoffrey Lewthwaite)*

A class 114 DMU at Barton on Humber, ready for the short journey to New Holland Pier on 24 June 1961.

(John Oxley)

Barton on Humber, 7 April 1983 with Hull – Scunthorpe and Scunthorpe – Hull buses both connecting with the Cleethorpes train.

(Martin Bairstow)

Barrow Haven, looking towards New Holland in April 1983. *(Martin Bairstow)*

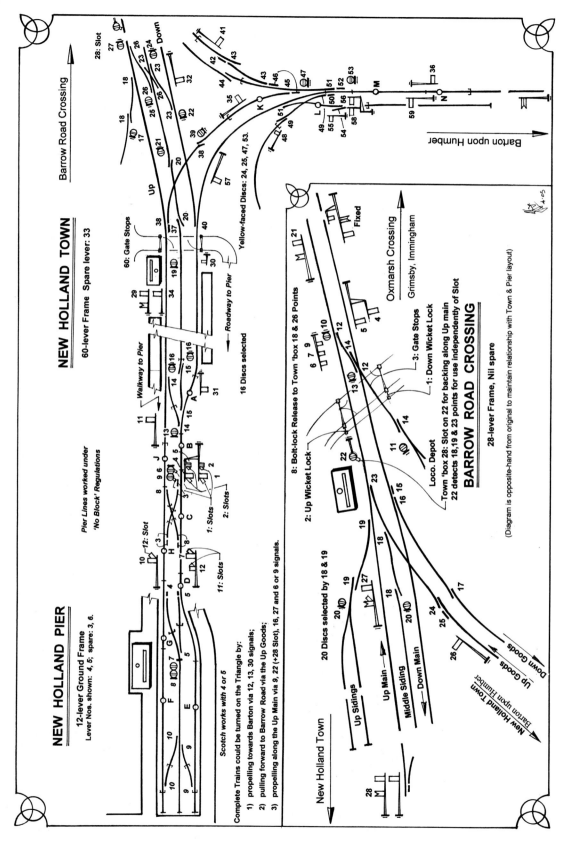

NEW HOLLAND PIER

12-lever Ground Frame
Lever Nos. shown: 4, 5; spare: 3, 6.

Pier Lines worked under
'No Block' Regulations

Scotch works with 4 or 5

Complete Trains could be turned on the Triangle by:

1) propelling towards Barton via 12, 13, 30 signals;
2) pulling forward to Barrow Road via the Up Goods;
3) propelling along the Up Main via 9, 22 (+28 Slot), 16, 27 and 6 or 9 signals.

10 – 12: Slot

11: Slots

1: Slots

2: Slots

NEW HOLLAND TOWN

60-lever Frame   Spare lever: 33

Barrow Road Crossing

Down

Up

Walkway to Pier

Roadway to Pier

60: Gate Stops

16 Discs selected

28: Slot

Yellow-faced Discs: 24, 25, 47, 53.

8: Bolt-lock Release to Town 'box 18 & 26 Points

Barton upon Humber

BARROW ROAD CROSSING

28-lever Frame, Nil spare

2: Up Wicket Lock

1: Down Wicket Lock

3: Gate Stops

Oxmarsh Crossing

Grimsby, Immingham

Loco. Depot

Town 'box 28: Slot on 22 for backing along Up main
22 detects 18,19 & 23 points for use independently of Slot

20 Discs selected by 18 & 19

New Holland Town

Up Sidings

Up Main

Middle Siding

Down Main

Up Goods

Down Goods

New Holland Town
Barton upon Humber

Fixed

(Diagram is opposite-hand from original to maintain relationship with Town & Pier layout)

Inside the wooden building at Barrow Haven. Accommodation was spartan but travellers were kept warm by the pot belly stove.
(Chris Bates)

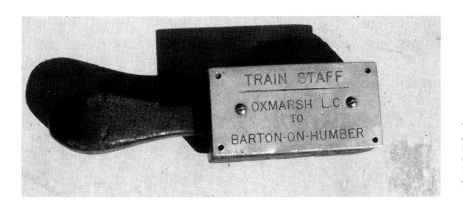

The train staff, which must be carried by any train venturing between Oxmarsh Level Crossing (New Holland) and Barton. This is instead of the earlier electric token working.
(Stuart Baker

The small 1981 station at New Holland, looking towards Barrow Road level crossing, where the Barton line branches left and the main line used to run out on to the pier.
(Stuart Baker)

The Humber Ferry

"The Booking Office in Nelson Street" is scarcely an adequate description and must predate construction, in 1880, of the station at Hull Corporation Pier.
(Geoffrey Lewthwaite)

The times shown leaving Hull are those at which the Steam Ferry leaves the Corporation Pier, and passengers having to book must present themselves at the Booking Office in Nelson Street at least three minutes before the times advertised for departure of the Steam Ferry, otherwise passengers cannot be booked; and should any delay from low tides or other cause beyond the Company's control occur in the passage of the Boats, the passengers must proceed from New Holland by the next available train.

So, for more than a Century, warned a footnote on every relevant page of the public timetable.

Since 1832, a small paddle steamer "Magna Charta" had been running between Hull and New Holland in competition with the longer established ferry to Barton. In January 1845, the New Holland ferry was purchased by the Provisional Committee of the Great Grimsby & Sheffield Junction Railway. Once the Railway had obtained its Act of incorporation, these Committee members made a personal profit by reselling the ferry to the Company of which they had just been appointed directors.

Powers for the Railway to operate the ferry were included in the same Act of July 1846, which had authorised the Barton branch. When the Railway opened to New Holland, on 1 March 1848, the ferry transferred to the pier head, where a floating pontoon was provided from December 1849.

Earlier that year, the Railway had purchased No 7 Nelson Street, which, for the next 132 years, served as Hull Corporation Pier Station. It was rebuilt in 1880. The MS&L did not invest in landing facilities in Hull, as permitted under the 1846 Act. Until about 1856, passengers and goods had sometimes to be offloaded into small boats, when the tide was too

low for the ferry to dock. The Railway then agreed to pay Hull Corporation for use of improved facilities at their pier, sometimes known as the Victoria Pier but more usually the Corporation Pier.

The Railway inherited four paddle steamers but quickly ordered new vessels of its own. The "Manchester" and "Sheffield" started a naming policy which later spread to the MS&L North Sea fleet. The first pair of ships proved unsatisfactory and, after five years, were replaced by new vessels with the same names.

The fleet was renewed in the Great Central era with the paddle steamer "Cleethorpes" of 1903 and the identical "Brocklesby" and "Killingholme" of 1912. These two were distinguished by their very tall funnels and by having a bow at each end. They were not symmetrical but could steam either way. At the start of the First World War, the three newest ships were requisitioned. Fortunately, two older vessels were still available to maintain the service. The three survived the War and continued until displaced from 1934 by the final generation of Humber paddle steamers.

Built at Hartlepool, the "Wingfield Castle" and "Tattersall Castle" were larger than their predecessors and able to carry cars, for which purpose the west side platform at New Holland was turned into a roadway. The similar "Lincoln Castle" was built in 1940 on the Clyde, from where it had to navigate submarine infested waters to reach the Humber.

The ferry was not always reliable. Low tides could cause delays and cancellations. At least these problems were predictable and known in advance. Fog was a far more serious obstacle. When the ferry was interrupted, New Holland used to telegraph other stations, who in turn passed the message on further so that, as far as possible, tickets were not issued to Hull whilst there was no way of getting there. In 1948, the paddle steamers were fitted with radar, after which fog became much less of a problem.

By the 1960s, the ferry was blighted by the promise of a Humber Bridge and the threat to close the connecting railways at New Holland. Two paddle steamers were withdrawn in 1972 -74. They were replaced by the ex Southern Railway diesel paddle vessel "Farringford". It was hoped that this and the "Lincoln Castle" would keep the service going until the bridge opened but construction was delayed and in 1978 the boilers of the "Lincoln Castle" were judged beyond economic repair. For the final three years, the "Farringford" alone maintained a reduced service, which ended on 24 June 1981, the day the Humber Bridge opened.

Besides passengers and cars, the ferry carried parcels, luggage in advance and most other sundries, traditionally associated with railway passenger services. For heavier freight, the Railway employed lighters, hauled by a steam tug. Until 1934, the LNER had its own tug "Barton". After that the towing was contracted out.

The "Yorkshire Belle"

The pleasure steamer Yorkshire Belle" was built in 1947 at Beverley and still runs coastal cruises out of Bridlington. During 1978 - 81, her then owners were contracted by BR to provide emergency cover for the "Farringford" during Winter overhaul and other absences. No cars could be carried but the passenger service was maintained.

The skipper of the "Yorkshire Belle" was Philip Thornton, who went on to become Bridlington's Harbour Master. He didn't have charge of her on

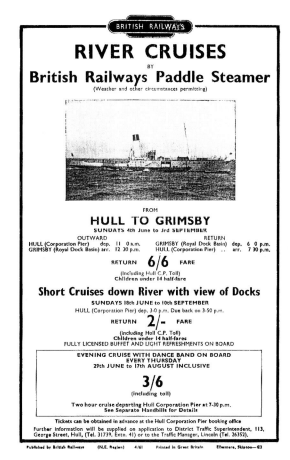

crossings from Hull to New Holland as BR put their own crews on board. A dent in her side below the water line survives as testimony to their navigational skill.

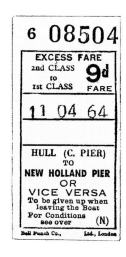

The "Lincoln Castle" depositing day trippers at the Royal Dock Basin, outside the lock gate, at Grimsby, about 1961.
(Peter Sunderland)

"But when the breezes blow".
On board the "Wingfield
Castle", May 1959.
(John Oxley)

"I generally go below". For a
supplement, discerning
passengers could "seek the
seclusion which a cabin
grants". "Lincoln Castle"
December 1972.
(John Holroyd)

But the true connoisseur
would be admiring the
polished brass work of the
engine room. "Tattersall
Castle" October 1970.
(John Holroyd)

The Hovercraft Experiment

The hovercraft was a British invention of the 1960s, which some people thought might usurp the traditional slow ferry. This never happened. The hovercraft has found plenty of military application but the only surviving passenger service is that between Southsea and Ryde, Isle of Wight, which has run since 1966.

In February 1969, Humber Hovercraft Services Ltd introduced two craft, "Mercury" and "Minerva" on a 30 minute schedule between Hull Corporation Pier and Grimsby Docks. They carried 65 passengers and up to five tons of cargo on four return trips each day. The journey time was a big advantage over the ferry and train via New Holland but the fare was at a premium. Operation was dogged by breakdowns and the service collapsed in October the same year.

Trying to bridge the Humber?

For 133 years, the Railway operated a paddle steamer across the Humber. Did it ever think of running a train? The answer seems to be yes but not very seriously.

The MS&L was present in Hull from 1848, but only via the ferry, which clearly had its limitations. Before planning a bridge or tunnel, the Company found ways of sending traffic round the Humber Estuary. On 1 August 1869, the North Eastern Railway opened its line between Thorne North and Staddlethorpe (now Gilberdyke) via Goole. On the same day, the MS&L opened the short connection between Stainforth Junction and Thorne North so that it could exercise running powers thence into Hull Paragon. Exactly five years later, the MS&L introduced an express passenger service between Liverpool and Hull by this route. Another five year interval saw the MS&L open its own goods terminal at Kingston Street, Hull on 1 August 1874. Most long distance traffic was finding its way round the Humber. Only from Lincolnshire did the ferry provide the sole means of reaching Hull.

During the 1880s, the MS&L and the North Eastern made trial borings on their respective sides of the Humber to try and determine the feasibility of a tunnel. In 1882, the two Companies opposed a Bill for an independent Hull & Lincoln Railway, which would have crossed the Humber on a bridge. They were determined that a Humber crossing should be under their control. By 1885, they were satisfied that a tunnel was feasible, but the North Eastern called for an end to further investigation. Their argument, which the MS&L accepted, was that the scheme had merit only as a defence against the promotion of competing railways.

In the view of the North Eastern, the experience of the Hull & Barnsley would be enough to put people off the idea of financing any further incursions into their territory. Consequently, they and the MS&L could afford to rely on their existing networks to serve Hull.

When a fixed link finally came in 1981, it was purely a road bridge.

The "Lincoln Castle" leaving New Holland on 27 December 1972.

(John Holroyd)

The Paddle Steamers "Grimsby" and "Cleethorpes" at New Holland Pier,
(Martin Bairstow Collection)

The "Farringford" arriving at New Holland on 20 April 1981. The diesel paddle vessel had been built in 1947 for the Lymington – Yarmouth service. It was named after Tennyson's home, now the Farringford Hotel, at Freshwater, Isle of Wight.
(Martin Bairstow)

"Minerva" in the Royal Dock basin at Grimsby in February 1969. The hovercraft service was a failure.
(Peter Sunderland)

Connections within Lincoln

A class 114 set negotiating Pelham Street en route from the diesel depot to Lincoln Central on 28 July 1979. It is crossing the Market Rasen to Lincoln St Marks line. Up until the late 1950s, the train would have been negotiating a road level crossing as well. *(G W Morrison)*

The MS&LR approached Lincoln both from Retford and from Barnetby but the Company never owned its own station in Lincoln. Until 1906, its two services used separate termini less than ¼ mile apart. From Barnetby direction, MS&L track extended almost to the entrance to both Lincoln stations. From Retford, the Company had to rely on running powers over the Great Northern Railway for the last seven miles into Lincoln Central.

The situation arose because the Sheffield & Lincolnshire Junction Railway, a constituent of the MS&L, wanted more or less the same route as that sought by the Great Northern Railway between Sykes Junction and Lincoln. Parliament adjudicated in favour of having the seven mile section built by the GN but with statutory running powers for the S&LJ.

The GN had been promoted in 1845 as the London & York Railway, with powers to build what is today the southern part of the East Coast Main Line. At Peterborough it spawned a subsidiary main line pointing almost due north through East Lincolnshire to Louth and Grimsby. A branch left that line at Boston heading northwest through Lincoln to Gainsborough. This line opened as far as Lincoln Central on 17 October 1848. It was extended to Gainsborough on 9 April 1849, exactly one week after the opening of the MS&L main line, with which it connected at Trent Junction. GN trains reversed here to reach the MS&L station, the present Gainsborough Central.

The MS&L Lincoln branch left the main line at Clarborough Junction, crossed the Trent at Torksey and joined the GN at Sykes Junction. It was ready for goods traffic by January 1850, but the GN prevented the MS&L from exercising its statutory running powers into Lincoln. For the time being the MS&L section did not open. But the GN had reciprocal running powers from Sykes Junction to Retford and, as soon as the branch was passed for passenger traffic, they wanted to use it. The GN advertised a service from 1 July 1850 but now it was the turn of the MS&L to block their line and keep the rival out. Common sense caught up with the situation on 7 August when the Clarborough Junction to Sykes Junction line opened to both passenger and goods traffic, MS&L and GN.

MS&L passenger trains ran through to the

Torksey looking towards Retford in August 1959.
(Geoffrey Lewthwaite)

station, which was known at first as Lincoln (GN). Under the LNER, it became Lincoln High Street and finally Lincoln Central. It was enlarged in 1883 and eventually reached eight platforms, four through and four bays at the east end, two of which have now disappeared to make a car park.

The station has always been difficult to operate because of the level crossings at each end. At the west end, the four platform lines and two through roads condense down to a double track over High Street level crossing. At the east end, eight platform lines and two through roads had to narrow to double track over Pelham Street level crossing, which was also traversed by a double track from Lincoln St Marks towards Market Rasen and by the curve from Central towards Market Rasen. At both High Street and Pelham Road, the gates had to be opened for shunting movements as well as for the timetabled arrival and departure of trains. It was not just road vehicles but pedestrians who were frustrated by the incessant operation of the crossings. About 1889, an eight feet wide footbridge was provided at Pelham Street, spanning all six tracks.

In the late 1950s, Pelham Street level crossing was replaced by a bridge, which was supposed to draw road traffic away from the High Street, where the level crossing is still in constant use today. Operation is easier with lifting barriers and there aren't the shunting movements which there used to be as all trains are DMU operated. Nowadays there is no track in platform 8, whilst the bay platforms 1 and 2 are under a car park. The rest of the station handles an average of five departures an hour. The layout is still controlled by semaphore signals.

The Joint Line

As already mentioned, the line between Gainsborough and Lincoln was built by the Great Northern Railway and might be outside the scope of this book but for it forming part of the MS&L route into Lincoln.

Once the MS&L had opened to Sykes Junction in 1850, the GN section thence to Gainsborough lost most of its importance. It closed at the end of November 1864, all GN traffic then going over the MS&L via Clarborough.

The closure was not permanent but was part of scheme to complete a cross country link between March and Doncaster. Under an Act of 1864, the Great Northern was empowered to build a new line from Trent West Junction, Gainsborough to Black Carr, south of Doncaster. At the same time, it was authorised to realign the route between Sykes Junction and what was to become Trent East Junction. Part of the cost was met by the Great Eastern Railway, which was trying to establish a direct link to the Yorkshire Coalfield in the hope of relieving its dependence on agricultural traffic in East Anglia. Both works were completed on 1 July 1867, the Great Eastern naturally exercising running powers to and beyond Doncaster. With immediate effect, the Great Northern ceased to use the MS&L between Sykes Junction and Retford. This cost the MS&L revenue but they were consoled with lump sum compensation under the 1864 Act, plus a fee for both GN and GE traffic using the MS&L viaduct between Trent East and West Junctions at Gainsborough.

The GN and GE enterprise was carried a further stage in 1882 with completion of a new line between Spalding and Pyewipe Junction, west of Lincoln. Built jointly, this included the Lincoln Avoiding Line, which passed round the south of the City, crossing the High Street on a bridge about $^3/_4$ mile south of the notorious level crossings. On 1 August 1882, a sum of money passed from the GE to the GN in return for which, the Pyewipe - Gainsborough - Black Carr section joined the rest of the route from March by becoming joint property. For the next 40 years, it was administered by a Joint Committee. This ceased to be necessary in 1923 when both Companies went the LNER. Yet even today, the route is still referred to

40143 passing Holmes West Junction, Lincoln on 28 July 1979 with a Saturdays Only Skegness to Manchester Piccadilly.
(G W Morrison)

as the Joint Line. It is still open apart from the March to Spalding section and the Lincoln Avoiding Line, both of which closed in 1983. There is now talk of diverting as much freight as possible away from the East Coast Main line between Peterborough and Doncaster because all the capacity is required by high speed passenger trains. Thanks to the demolition of the Lincoln Avoiding Line, this is going to involve a lot more train movement over High Street Level Crossing.

Sykes Junction

The signal box was opened in 1885, by which time the line was under GN GE Joint ownership. The box was a GN installation but the design owed something to the GE boxes further south on the Joint Line. It had an 18 lever McKenzie & Holland frame.

Sykes Junction was a reporting box, which meant that the signalman had to notify details of passing trains to both Lincoln and Doncaster controls. Despite having amalgamated in 1923, the former Great Central and Great Northern lines retained their different systems of communication. The former had an omnibus circuit telephone, the latter a single needle telegraph. To use the omnibus circuit, you were supposed to pick up the phone, listen to see if anyone was already on, if necessary wait and then press the code, for the place you were trying to ring.

The single needle telegraph was similar in appearance to a block instrument with dial upon which a needle moved to the left for a dot and to the right for a dash. At the same time, it made a sharp sound for the dot and a flat tone for the dash. The "reader" could watch the needle, listen to the tones or both according to preference and experience. Messages were sent in Morse by turning a handle at the base of the machine. Each signal box, or other location had a call sign, on hearing which, the incumbent would respond by repeating it back. The sender would then identify himself with his own call sign. The recipient would then give a T or a G according to his level of confidence in receiving Morse. T meant break it up with spaces between words. G meant send it without any breaks.

Mr D G Crosby worked Sykes Junction box from March 1957 until closure of the branch in November 1959. On nights, he often had difficulty conducting traffic business on the Great Central omnibus circuit

61867 negotiating the curved platform through Gainsborough Lea Road with the 9.36 (Mondays and Fridays only) from March to Manchester Central on 1 August 1960. This station gained a much better train service with the closure of Torksey Viaduct in 1959.
(David Holmes)

Lea, the first station south of Gainsborough on the Joint Line. *(Alan Young collection)*

Stow Park looking towards Gainsborough. It was known as Marton until 1871.
(Alan Young collection)

Passing Sykes Junction box. The signal is pulled off for the Joint Line towards Gainsborough.

(R J Goodman)

Class B1 No61050 calls at Saxilby with a train from Lincoln Central to Retford on 9 August 1959.

(Geoffrey Lewthwaite)

Class B1 No 61327 beside the River Witham near Pyewipe Junction on 25 July 1959.

(Martin Bairstow collection)

A DMU at Lincoln St Marks on 7 April 1984.

(Martin Bairstow)

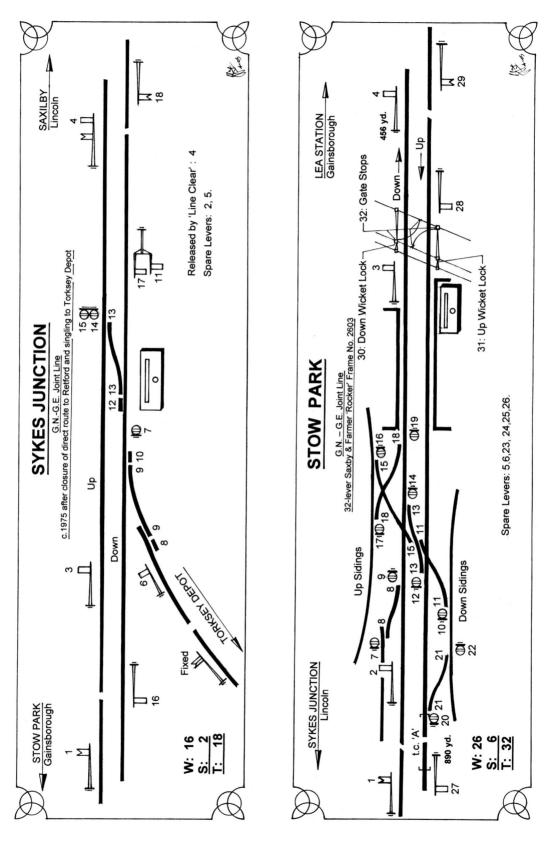

SYKES JUNCTION

G.N.-G.E. Joint Line

c.1975 after closure of direct route to Retford and singling to Torksey Depot

SAXILBY
Lincoln

STOW PARK
Gainsborough

Up

Down

TORKSEY DEPOT

Fixed

Released by 'Line Clear' : 4

Spare Levers: 2, 5.

W: 16
S: 2
T: 18

STOW PARK

G.N. – G.E. Joint Line

32-lever Saxby & Farmer 'Rocker' Frame No. 2603

LEA STATION
Gainsborough

456 yd.

SYKES JUNCTION
Lincoln

Up

Down

32: Gate Stops

30: Down Wicket Lock

31: Up Wicket Lock

Up Sidings

Down Sidings

t.c. 'A'

890 yd.

Spare Levers: 5,6,23, 24,25,26.

W: 26
S: 6
T: 32

as the line could be occupied for long periods with chatter about football and other topics with which the various signalmen passed the lonely hours. But there were no such problems on the Great Northern circuit as nobody was likely to be talking football on the telegraph.

The usual block section from Sykes Junction was to Leverton. The signalman had a list of running times for all trains from class A (express passenger) downwards. This determined how long he must wait, after receiving "train on line" from Leverton, before offering it forward and clearing his signals. If he did this too soon, he might delay traffic on the Joint Line (Lincoln to Gainsborough). The time for a class E freight was 18 minutes but, on one occasion in the early hours of the morning, one actually took 40 minutes causing delay to a parcels train on the Joint Line. Mr Crosby had to report and explain why the parcels train had been held at his signal. He heard nothing more about it so assumes that attention was turned to the driver of the freight.

Sykes Junction was open continuously from 3am on Monday until passage of the Mottram to Lincoln goods in the early hours of Sunday morning. It reopened during Sunday as required by the passenger service and any excursions and main line diversions. During bad weather Mr Crosby might go there on Sunday evening, get a fire going and sleep rather than make his way to a frozen box at 3am. On one occasion, after a heavy snow fall in 1958, he could only get to Sykes Junction by catching a train from Saxilby Station.

In the 1950s, there were six stopping passenger trains to and from the Great Central line, mostly from Sheffield Victoria to Lincoln Central. Prestige train of the day was the Continental Boat Train, through from Liverpool Central to Harwich Town, which passed Sykes Junction about 4.25pm eastbound and just before midday on the return, when it ran non stop from Lincoln Central to Sheffield Victoria.

There were only four passenger trains year round on a Sunday but in Summer, there were the "Fishermen's Trains", also referred to as "Anglers Excursions". These were of long standing. In Summer 1935, three trains originated at Wadsley Bridge, west of Sheffield. They passed Sykes Junction at 7.59, 8.25 and 8.33 am bound respectively for Surfleet, Midville and Boston. They passed on the return at 7.48, 7.58 and 8.10pm, having afforded a good days fishing to parties of anglers from the South Yorkshire conurbation. Two of the trains ran only June to September, but the third continued well into November but with an earlier return time, reflecting the shorter day light.

Sykes Junction was busiest during the strawberry picking season when a night shift could fill 1½ pages of both train register and telegraph book. Fruit trains headed north on the Joint Line from Whitemoor Yard, March. The even reporting numbers were for Doncaster and beyond, the odd ones for the GC line.

About 1957, Torksey Viaduct was hit by a barge, causing rail traffic to be reduced to one track over

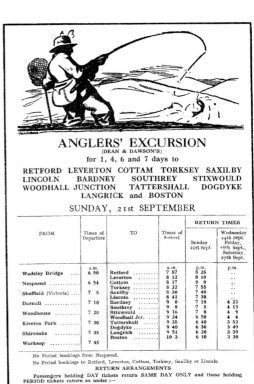

ANGLERS' EXCURSION
(DEAN & DAWSON'S)
for 1, 4, 6 and 7 days to

RETFORD LEVERTON COTTAM TORKSEY SAXILBY
LINCOLN   BARDNEY   SOUTHREY   STIXWOULD
WOODHALL JUNCTION   TATTERSHALL   DOGDYKE
LANGRICK and BOSTON

SUNDAY, 21st SEPTEMBER

FROM	Times of Departure	TO	Times of Arrival	RETURN TIMES	
				Sunday 21st Sept.	Wednesday 24th Sept., Friday, 26th Sept., Saturday, 27th Sept.
	a.m.		a.m.	p.m.	p.m.
Wadsley Bridge	6 50	Retford	7 57	8 25	..
		Leverton	8 12	8 10	..
Neepsend	6 54	Cottam	8 17	8 0	..
		Torksey	8 22	7 55	..
Sheffield (Victoria)	7 5	Saxilby	8 30	7 40	..
		Lincoln	8 41	7 30	..
Darnall	7 10	Bardney	9 0	7 19	4 22
		Southrey	9 8	7 5	4 13
Woodhouse	7 20	Stixwould	9 16	7 0	4 9
		Woodhall Jct.	9 24	6 50	4 4
Kiveton Park	7 30	Tattershall	9 35	6 40	3 52
		Dogdyke	9 40	6 30	3 49
Shireoaks	7 35	Langrick	9 51	6 20	3 39
Worksop	7 45	Boston	10 3	6 10	3 30

No Period bookings from Neepsend.
No Period bookings to Retford, Leverton, Cottam, Torksey, Saxilby or Lincoln

RETURN ARRANGEMENTS

Passengers holding DAY tickets return SAME DAY ONLY and those holding
PERIOD tickets return as under :—
4 Days—Wednesday 24th September.   6 Days—Friday, 26th September
7 Days—Saturday, 27th September
at the times shown above.
FOR FARES, CONDITIONS OF ISSUE, etc., SEE OTHER SIDE

London & North Eastern Railway

the damaged structure. At first, pilotman working was used until electric token machines were installed in Cottam and Torksey boxes. Previously, these had been switched out except when the pick up goods wanted to shunt but now they had to be manned during all hours that trains ran. The arrangement was short lived as the Clarborough to Sykes Junction section closed on 1 November 1959. At the request of the Gainsborough Model Railway Society, the last local passenger trains, the 7.20pm (Sundays) Lincoln Central to Retford and 8.55pm return were hauled by a clean Class J11 no 64318 in place of the usual DMU but the very last train was B1 no 61248 on a return excursion from Manchester to Cambridge. Sykes Junction continued as a block post, with slightly shorter opening hours.

One track was quickly removed between Sykes Junction and Torksey but the other was used for wagon storage until 1965. On 31 January 1966, this stretch reopened to serve the oil terminal at Torksey. Traffic came from Stanlow, Saltend (near Hull) and Immingham but ceased during 1988, causing both the branch and Sykes Junction box to close on 18 September.

Between Clarborough Junction and Cottam, both lines were used for wagon storage until about 1964 when work started on the coal fired power station at Cottam. The line reopened in 1968 and is still operating.

Only the section between Cottam and Torksey

After closure in 1959, the section between Sykes Junction and Torksey was used for wagon storage.
(R J Goodman)

The "gallows" were a familiar sight guarding the exit from goods yards, ensuring that wagons were not laden beyond the loading gauge.
(R J Goodman)

To facilitate "merry go round" working, the line from Clarborough Junction ends in a loop at Cottam. This is being traversed by a DMU railtour in October 1989. *(Stuart Baker)*

Torksey Viaduct, 45 years after closure. *(Martin Bairstow)*

Brayford Pool, Lincoln with class J6 No 64260 heading towards Central Station, about 1957. *(A M Ross)*

A DMU negotiating High Street level crossing as it departs Lincoln Central for Doncaster in 1979.
(Tom Heavyside)

remained permanently closed from 1959. The viaduct is still in position and may eventually open as a cycle track,

The passenger service between Sheffield, Retford and Lincoln Central was diverted via Gainsborough Lea Road. Since 1998, it has operated at an hourly interval.

Lincoln St Marks

Approaching Lincoln, the Barnetby line crossed the Great Northern Railway on the level before making end on connection with the Midland Railway at the latter Company's station. It was only in 1950, that this station was given the suffix St Marks. It was the older of the two Lincoln Stations, having opened on 3 August 1846 as the terminus of the Midland Railway branch from Nottingham. It became a through station with the arrival of the MS&L on 18 December 1849. The four tracks were flanked by two platforms and spanned by an overall roof. The main building, in classical style, ran parallel to the platforms on the north side. MS&L trains crossed the High Street by a level crossing, just a short distance south of that on the Great Northern.

Shortly after the opening, a curve was built connecting the MS&L to the Great Northern. This meant that traffic from Market Rasen could run into either the Midland or the Great Northern station. Until 31 March 1906, normal passenger trains all went to the Midland.

From 1 April 1906, the Great Central transferred its Market Rasen line trains into the Great Northern Station. This left Lincoln Midland with a regular passenger service only from Nottingham. Apart from transfer movements and seaside specials, it was possible to work the station almost as a terminus, keeping to a minimum, use of the level crossing over the High Street.

By 1962, St Marks enjoyed an almost hourly service to Nottingham, mostly DMU operated. The route was listed for closure in the Beeching Report, but the threat was soon lifted.

Instead, on 1 March 1965, BR opened a new south to east curve at Newark, giving access to Lincoln St Marks from the East Coast Main Line. The idea was that this would facilitate closure of both the ex GN line from Grantham to Lincoln Central and also the East Lincolnshire line from Boston to Grimsby.

Freight began to be diverted straight away. Passenger trains followed on 1 November 1965, when the Market Rasen service was transferred back to St Marks in order that this should become the main route between London and Grimsby. Intermediate stations on the Market Rasen line had closed two days earlier. They were all at remote locations apart from Reepham, which is now in the midst of significant population.

There was pressure both within and without the Railway Industry to remove the duplicate station facilities at Lincoln, not to mention the duplicate level crossings. The problem was that trains could not get into Central Station from the Nottingham/Newark line until 1985 when the tight 20 mph curve was built between Boultham and West Holmes Junctions. St Marks Station closed on 11 May.

Since then, the site has been redeveloped into the St Marks Shopping Centre, which adopts a purple totem sign as its corporate image. The former station building won the 1997 Ian Allan Heritage award for the best restoration project no longer in railway use. The management office is in the shape of a signal box, with an authentic purple enamel sign proclaiming "British Railways St Marks Station".

The through London to Cleethorpes service finished in May 1993. Connections from London to Lincoln are available at Newark North Gate. Whilst some of these trains continue to Grimsby Town, it is often quicker to go via Doncaster, if you want to travel from London to Barnetby, Habrough, Grimsby Town or Cleethorpes.

The main entrance to Lincoln St Marks Station. Since closure, the building has been incorporated into the retail development. *(John Oxley)*

03021 heading towards Pelham Street from Lincoln St Marks on 7 October 1976, passing the former Great Central Railway East Goods Yard. *(Tom Heavyside)*

37042 taking the curve into Lincoln Central in 1976 with steel from Scunthorpe which will have reversed at Barnetby. Beyond the diesel depot is the loco works of Ruston Hornsby. *(Tom Heavyside)*

Reepham, the first station out of Lincoln in June 1962.
(Geoffrey Lewthwaite)

Langworth box in April 1993. Dating from 1890, it had its lever frame replaced by a panel in 1990. *(Alan Young)*

Wickenby box in April 2003. Both box and panel are of the same vintage as Langworth.
(Alan Young)

Market Rasen Station with long demolished overall roof.
(Dave Enefer collection)

Moortown for Caistor in January 1961. The township of Caistor, 2½ miles distant, lies on the edge of the Lincolnshire Wolds. A branch to Caistor was authorised by the GG&SJ Act of 1846, but it was never built.
(Geoffrey Lewthwaite)

The main building at Moortown in 2003.
(Alan Young)

Snelland looking north on a dull day in January 1961. The station served only a small village and closed in 1965.
(Geoffrey Lewthwaite)

Class B1 No 61348 approaching Holton Le Moor from the south on 17 September 1960.
(Martin Bairstow collection)

North Kelsey Station. The village was 1½ miles to the west.
(Alan Young collection)

Barnetby looking east on 27 April 1968.
(Geoffrey Lewthwaite)

Welham Road and Clarborough Junction

Mr I J Wilkinson lived close to the line at Welham Road, where his family owned some grazing land on either side of the Railway. They also rented an additional piece of land belonging to the Railway until 1989, when Mr Wilkinson bought it. With the land, he acquired documents which showed that part had been conveyed to the MS&L in 1847 by Thomas Wheelwright. The other part had been conveyed in 1852 by five joint owners including Cassandra Gylby and Wo rthington Thomas Gylby, what fascinating Dickensian names. The following paragraphs are from Mr Wilkinson's notes.

Welham Road was an 11 lever box with two spare. It had two sidings, to which up to five wagons could be propelled from Thrumpton - a job usually carried out by the banker. Between Thrumpton and Welham was Gringley Road box where drivers gave a whistle to indicate their route beyond Clarborough - one long for the main line, three short for the Lincoln branch. Gringley Road then gave an extra beat on the block bell after "train on line" for branch trains. This was passed on by Welham Road to Clarborough Junction box.

At Clarborough Junction, there were two signalman's cottages, reached by a small bridge over a dyke off Rat Hole Lane. Demolished in the 1950s, they were similar in style to those still visible at Rushey Siding, west of Retford, which have been conve rted into one privately owned dwelling. I clearly remember a signalman who lived in one of the cottages for many years. He had been a soldier, s e rving under Baden Powell at the relief of Mafeking. Because of staff shortages during and after the Second World War, he had been kept on into his seventies. He was not sociable and did not welcome S&T engineers into his box. Firemen carrying out Rule 55 were also treated with hostility. For many years there was a splitting distant on the up line but, eventually this was replaced by a single arm, kept at caution for Lincoln bound trains.

Clarborough Junction was a summit, approached from all three directions by a three mile climb, mostly at 1 in 120. From Retford, the climb was virtually unbroken until it eased to 1 in 243 through Clarborough Tunnel. It was in this direction that loaded coal trains required the assistance of the Clarborough banker, also known as the Low Yard or Thrumpton pilot.

My first memories are of J10 0 - 6 - 0s 5141,5807 and 5808 coming on at Thrumpton or Welham Road. Later came the J5s, 3022, 3023 and 3028. Post War bankers included classes J3, J21 and J52 but the saddle tanks did not stay long as their brake power left something to be desired in the event of a train becoming divided.

There was also a night banker, often a C2 as several of the remaining small "Atlantics" were shedded at Retford. Once, when I was at Welham Road, the banker, a J5, was sent to Leverton to assist an ailing C1 up to Clarborough. The J5 remained on

A class WD 2 – 8 – 0 with a down freight approaching Rat Hole Lane crossing. The flat roof signal box at Clarborough Junction is just visible in the background.

(I J Wilkinson)

to Retford. The young fireman seemed to be having a white knuckle ride as he passed Welham Road on the downgrade. When wartime traffic was heavy, a banker was provided on a Sunday. The type of loco varied. I can even remember a B7 on one of these duties.

The Grimsby to Leicester Fish Express passed Welham Road about 2pm. Three coaches and 18 to 25 fish vans were usually hauled by a four cylinder B3 or B7 or a "Sam Fay" B2. It returned early evening with the three passenger coaches only.

Frodingham coke trains had to reverse at Barnetby so they frequently sported a brake van at each end. Lime traffic was often conveyed in private owner wagons of the Steetley Lime & Basic Company whose main premises were between Worksop and Whitwell.

An evening trip from Retford to Gainsborough consisted of engine and brake only on the out run but returned with products from Marshall Engineering Works at Gainsborough. I have seen general purpose engines, steam rollers, portable engines, threshing drums and elevators amongst the loads. Once, during the War, I was in Welham Road box when this train passed with an out of gauge load, heavily sheeted down. I believe it was a midget submarine, of which a number were constructed at Marshalls.

A light engine passed Welham Road each morning en route to shunt Gainsborough Lea Road.

For a number of years, it was a Y3 Sentinel crewed by a driver and shunter. It returned about 5.30pm. Most of the ex GC 4 - 6 - 0 types would appear on excursions, including B8s. In post war years, some of the specials consisted of LMS locos and stock. "Crabs", 4Fs and occasional 3Fs were noted.

Local passenger trains were usually hauled by D2s, D3s or D9s, though sometimes the Retford based B4 would appear. Pre war, a C13 tank engine ran from Sheffield to Lincoln each morning with three compartment coaches. When the train returned, the loco had always been turned at Lincoln. Otherwise, tank engines were rare. The prestige train of the day was the Harwich Parkeston Quay to Liverpool Central which passed on the down at about 12 noon and up at about 3pm. The locos I most remember were the B17 class of which 2845 "The Suffolk Regiment" was a frequent performer. On the down, there was an early evening passenger to Sheffield from East Anglia which carried some exotic roofboards. A Saturday morning horse box special would pass on its way from Aintree to Newmarket. This I eagerly awaited as it was always drawn by a D16, as yet unrebuilt with plenty of gleaming brasswork. The Retford to Lincoln pick up goods ran daily. Cottam and Torksey boxes were opened, if required, by the porter signalmen.

In the event of serious trouble on the East Coast Main Line, trains between Retford and Grantham were rerouted via Sykes Junction and Lincoln. I saw my first V2 2 - 6 - 2 on one of these occasions.

Leverton signal box. The level crossing on what is now the Cottam Power Station branch is worked as an automatic half barrier. *(I J Wilkinson)*

A class O1 2 – 8 – 0 leaving Clarborough Tunnel with an eastbound coal train in September 1963. *(I J Wilkinson)*

The western ventilating shaft above the 656 yard Clarborough Tunnel. *(I J Wilkinson)*

Cottam station and signal box, August 1959.
(Geoffrey Lewthwaite)

Relief Booking Clerk

Paul Needham began his railway career in 1956 and was, from 1958, a relief booking clerk based at Gainsborough covering a wide area from Kiveton Bridge to Barnetby. He ended up a Parcels Manager at Leeds and now, in retirement, volunteers on the Strathspey Railway in Scotland. The following memories are taken from his notes.

The Gainsborough Station Master covered both Central and Lea Road, where he lived in the Station House. His grade was Special Class C. Central Station had a pilot loco from Retford Shed on a two shift basis. Lea Road had a pilot only in the grain season. The Central loco covered during the rest of the year, making a daily trip between the two stations around mid day.

Marshall, Sons & Co (later Marshall – Fowler) had private sidings at Central, which they shunted with their own loco. If this was out of service, a BR engine was sent from Retford, usually a 0 – 4 – 0 Sentinel.

During slack periods, and when the Station Master had gone home, some poaching activity took place between Gainsborough and Thurock Siding using the pilot engine and a brake van. Gainsborough Central goods required no relief clerk as it had sufficient staff to cover holidays and sickness. The Station Master had his own clerk whose job was mainly on personnel matters, though not staff rostering. On Mondays, it was all go working out staff timesheets for paybills, deducting PAYE and sticking stamps on the National Insurance cards. I was never very keen on this job as you were under the beady eye of the SM for most of the day and woe betide if any mistakes were made, particularly any underpayments when it came to pay day.

Late turn Saturday was a shift that I quite enjoyed. Everything was quiet, most passengers having already gone out for the day in Sheffield for football or shopping or, during the Summer, to Cleethorpes. Saturday afternoon was a time to visit the "Horse & Groom" with the crew off the pilot, including guard and shunter. On one of these occasions, the driver and a trainee were left behind to deal with a horse box, which was to be detached from a train from Sheffield. Unfortunately, they managed to derail the horsebox. A hurried call was made to the pub to recall the rest of the staff who had to purchase onions to cover the smell of beer before the SM arrived and re-railing commenced.

On another occasion, a new porter, keen to learn clerical duties was left in charge whilst the rest of us again went down to the Horse & Groom. At the end of the shift, I found we had a surplus of £3 10s. Any loss or surplus over £1 had to be reported and this was duly done. I had been covering for the chief clerk who informed me, a few days later, that there had been £5 extra in the float on Saturday and so my £3 10s "surplus" was in fact a £1 10s loss. I was then subjected to enquiry by the Passenger Commercial Assistant and a Personnel Assistant, both from Doncaster, out for the day on expenses costing more than my loss. They suggested that, as a young married man with two small sons, I might be short

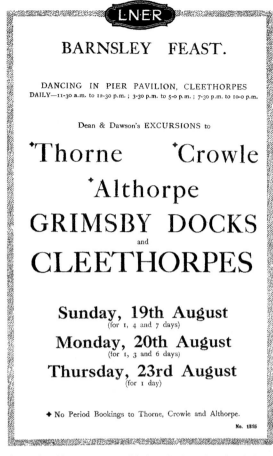

of cash. No way could I admit who had been manning the office whilst I was in the Pub so I bluffed my way out suggesting that the interview be continued with a trade union official present. At that point they terminated the enquiry telling me that a relief clerk should know better, being more experienced than a mere station clerk.

Gainsborough Central boasted a Refreshment Room. On Summer Sundays, most excursions stopped for water both out and return. Whilst this was happening, the Refreshment Room team – an S & T engineer and his wife plus the on duty porter – would be serving ice cream as fast as they could. The enterprise came to an end when the S & T man was jailed for selling copper wire to the local scrap merchants. As far as was known, his wife moved back to her parents in Doncaster and the Refreshment Room closed.

Subsequently, one of the long serving porters, Ernest Stainton took me into the derelict Refreshment Room where lockers had been removed to reveal a flight of stairs. This led up to a large room, which had been used for meetings, possibly by senior officers of the MS&L out for the day on expenses.

The Station Master at Kirton Lindsey was minus one hand, which he was reputed to have lost in the Home Guard whilst complaining about having to train with "unarmed" hand grenades. The station was not very busy on the passenger side until Friday and Saturday when it became inundated with RAF National Service types, going on leave. On late turn Monday to Thursday, you rarely took more than £5 but on Friday it could be in excess of £1,000. At Bank Holidays, a special train started westbound from Kirton Lindsey. Most travelled on warrants, which had to be exchanged for Forces Duty tickets. To prevent delays at the station, a supply of blank tickets was taken up to the Camp and a tressle table set up in a cell in the Guard Room, to which recruits were marched in one by one.

I never relieved at Blyton, nor at Scawby & Hibaldstow which had no clerical staff. Tickets there would be issued by a porter.

From Brigg, a cheap day return to Grimsby Docks cost 5s 10d. Sleepers were sold as firewood at 1s 2d each. I sold five sleepers for 5s 10d but forgot to enter the sum in the daily cash return. At the month end, I inadvertently carried forward the wrong serial number for cheap day returns to Grimsby Docks – by one ticket. So the books appeared to balance.

Then the auditors arrived, discovered the ticket error and started to tear the place apart. They found a pad of paper tickets, MS&L Railway privilige exchange vouchers for use in conjunction with the South Eastern Railway for Continental travel. Only two had ever been used, the last one in 1888. My predecessor from 70 years earlier should have needed these to balance. I wonder how he explained away his shortage. The auditors were so pleased with their historic find that they never commented on my sloppy working.

Saxilby had a Station Master who, with so little to do, went in for car repairs. On one occasion, he was under a car when an Officers` Special arrived. He didn`t know who he was talking to when a voice (the District Superintendent) asked where the Station Master was. It took some explaining.

The same fellow was responsible for Sykes Junction box. He failed to report a defective step leading up to the box. The signalmen were aware of it but an unfortunate Doncaster freight guard wasn`t and he fell into the large water butt under the steps whilst trying to carry out Rules and Regulations with his train at a stand during the night.

By the 1950s, Gainsborough Central had long lost its overall roof, replaced by platform canopies.
(Dave Enefer collection)

opposite page upper K3 No 61939 passing Grimsby Docks with the 4.30pm fish to Whitland on 14 June 1962.
(Roger Hockney)

opposite page lower 79051 at Barton on Humber, shortly after dieselisation in July 1956. These early Metro Cammell sets, all second class, were withdrawn by 1969. They never acquired a class number. *(Colour rail)*

Brigg had also once boasted an overall roof. The view towards Barnetby in the 1960s.
(Martin Bairstow collection)

The Trent, Ancholme & Grimsby Railway

A Cleethorpes to Sheffield DMU restarts on 4 May 1987 from Crowle Central, where the main station building was on the south side of the canal, accessed by a swing bridge.   *(G W Morrison)*

Strictly, the title applies only to the section between the Keadby and Barnetby but is used here to describe the route across North Lincolnshire, which has eclipsed the earlier more southerly MS&L main line.

Nowadays, the main passenger service is the hourly "Trans Pennine Express" between Manchester Airport, Sheffield and Cleethorpes. At first sound, this might be the direct successor to the expresses of the Manchester, Sheffield & Lincolnshire Railway. But not until they reach Barnetby, do these trains touch the former MS&L main line. Between Manchester and Sheffield, they are obliged to take the Midland route through the Hope Valley because the MS&L Woodhead Line is closed. East of Sheffield, they are drawn by commercial instinct to go via Doncaster and Scunthorpe, rather than the traditional route route through Gainsborough and Brigg.

Apart from Doncaster Station, the present route is ex MS&L all the way from Mexborough to Cleethorpes. It was not planned as a single entity, but was built piecemeal. It was completed in 1866 with the opening of the Trent, Ancholme & Grimsby Railway between Keadby and Barnetby.

The line between Mexborough and Doncaster

was opened on 10 November 1849 by the South Yorkshire Railway. This organisation was leased by the MS&L in 1864 and fully absorbed ten years later. Its original full name was the South Yorkshire, Doncaster & Goole Railway. This changed in April 1850 to the South Yorkshire Railway and River Dun Navigation Company, when the Railway took over the local canal interests.

The first line from Doncaster to Thorne was built, without Parliamentary powers, alongside the canal. Opened for goods on 11 December 1855, the single track included some very sharp curves with severe speed restrictions. None the less, a passenger service of two trains a day began on 1 July 1856. Shortly afterwards, the Railway purchased a steamer to ply along the canal from Thorne to Keadby, where connection could be made into the Gainsborough & Hull Steam Packets, plying along the Trent.

The canal steamer was no longer required when the Railway extended from Thorne to Keadby on 10 September 1859. Again, this was done without Parliamentary powers, alongside the canal, which followed a fairly straight course, once it had reached the first station at Mauds Bridge. Thorne Station was moved 1/4 mile east of the original terminus at Thorne Lock. At Keadby, the line had reached the natural

Medge Hall looking towards Doncaster. This remote station closed in September 1960.
(Alan Young collection)

The 1885 signal box at Appleby (Lincs). After two years with a temporary portakabin, the box was refurbished and brought back into use in 2005.
(F W Smith)

The down platform at Crowle Central in July 1974. Access to the main building, extreme left, involved crossing the canal on a swing bridge but the station had been unstaffed since 1969.　*(Alan Young)*

A B1 crossing Keadby Bridge with a Doncaster to Cleethorpes passenger train on 26 June 1960. *(John Oxley)*

Class O2 No 63957 comes off the Keadby Lifting Bridge with coal for Frodingham on 25 October 1961. The lower level line in the foreground was connected to the pre 1916 swing bridge. *(John Oxley)*

WD 2 – 8 – 0 No 90506 attacks Gunhouse Bank with assistance in the rear, about 1960. *(John Oxley)*

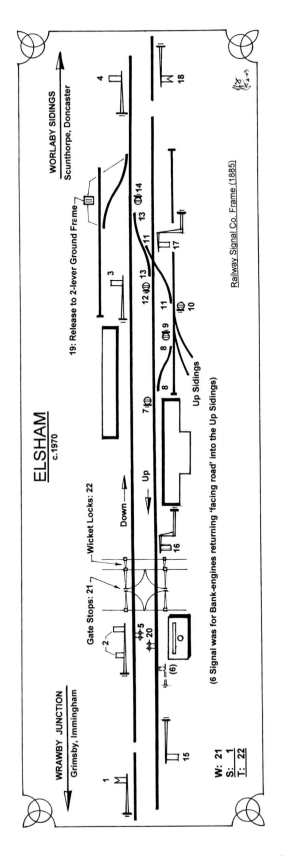

ELSHAM
c.1970

WORLABY SIDINGS
Scunthorpe, Doncaster

WRAWBY JUNCTION
Grimsby, Immingham

19: Release to 2-lever Ground Frame

Down →

← Up

Up Sidings

Wicket Locks: 22

Gate Stops: 21

(6) Signal was for Bank-engines returning 'facing road' into the Up Sidings)

Railway Signal Co. Frame (1885)

W: 21
S: 1
T: 22

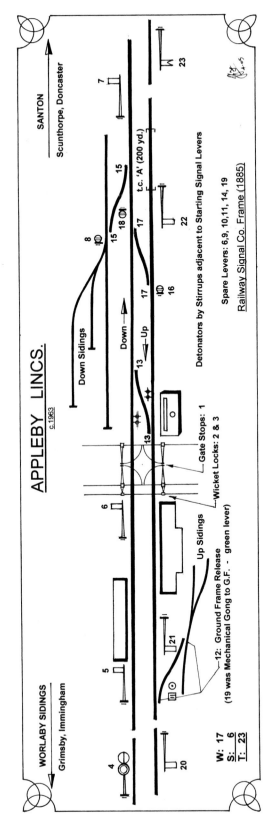

APPLEBY LINCS.
c.1963

SANTON
Scunthorpe, Doncaster

WORLABY SIDINGS
Grimsby, Immingham

Down Sidings

Down

Up

t.c. 'A' (200 yd.)

Up Sidings

Gate Stops: 1

Wicket Locks: 2 & 3

12: Ground Frame Release
(19 was Mechanical Gong to G.F. – green lever)

Detonators by Stirrups adjacent to Starting Signal Levers

Spare Levers: 6,9, 10,11, 14, 19

Railway Signal Co. Frame (1885)

W: 17
S: 6
T: 23

barrier of the River Trent, which was sufficient goal for the time being.

The incentive to bridge the waterway came with the discovery of iron ore deposits in the area, which was destined to develop as Scunthorpe.

Authorised in July 1861, the Trent, Ancholme & Grimsby Railway was promoted jointly by the MS&L and the South Yorkshire. A third of the cost was subscribed by Rowland Winn, who had the good fortune to own the estate under which the ore had been found. The Act provided for an exchange of running powers, the MS&L gaining access to the South Yorkshire coalfield and the South Yorkshire to the Port of Grimsby. Running powers became academic when the South Yorkshire was leased to the MS&L before the new line opened.

The TA&G began at Gunhouse Wharf on the east bank of the Trent, facing but unconnected to the existing terminus at Keadby. A separate Act authorised the 2¼ mile link between Keadby and Gunhouse Junctions, crossing the Trent by a swing bridge. Work was completed in time for a Directors' special on 1 July 1864 but there was a long delay before the route was completed to the satisfaction of the Board of Trade. The line opened for goods, through to Barnetby on 1 May 1866 and to passengers on the following 1 October. The main engineering feature, besides the swing bridge, was the 85 arch Scotter Road Viaduct, 1,020 yards in length, built entirely in brick.

At first there were just two trains each way, weekdays only. Stations at Althorpe, Frodingham, Appleby and Elsham all had staggered platforms. Frodingham stood immediately east of Brigg Road level crossing. It was replaced by a structure west of the crossing in 1887. An additional station opened at Gunness, just east of Keadby Bridge in 1869. The original Keadby Station, bypassed by the new line, remained open for passengers until 31 October 1874 after which the short stub continued as a goods branch.

Between Doncaster and Mauds Bridge, the sinuous single track alongside the canal was no use for the heavy traffic anticipated from the extension beyond Keadby. Under powers obtained in 1861, the South Yorkshire let contracts in November 1864 for 9½ miles of well aligned double track to bypass the earlier route. The new alignment opened on 1 October 1866, with replacement stations at Barnby Dun, Stainforth & Hatfield and Thorne but not at Bramwith or Mauds Bridge. Between Mauds Bridge and Keadby, the canal was fairly straight so most of the railway alignment was satisfactory, requiring only to be widened from single to double track. Powers for this were obtained in 1866 but work did not begin until 1870. It was completed on 20 November 1871. The new alignment leaves the canal briefly between Medge Hall and Godnow Bridge.

Keadby Bridge

The Railway crossed the Trent by a bridge 484 ft in length, including an opening section of 160ft. There were three fixed spans on the Althorpe side of the moveable section and one on the Gunness side. The signal box stood immediately west of the opening span, which placed it near the centre of the bridge. Rising above the box, was a signal post with two lower quadrant arms, facing river traffic from the two directions. These were "pulled off" when the bridge was swung open for a ship to pass.

By 1910, the swing bridge was in need of considerable expenditure. There was need for a road bridge further north than Gainsborough. With extra rail traffic expected from Immingham, the Great Central deposited a Bill for a 5¼ mile deviation all the way from Keadby to Frodingham, including a lifting bridge for road and rail some ¾ mile north of the existing swing bridge. The Bill attracted little

The sliding bridge at Keadby Canal Junction, open to canal traffic on 6 April 1974.
(John Holroyd)

70

The original terminus at Keadby, bypassed when the line was extended across the Trent. Still in use for goods in June 1960. *(John Oxley)*

opposition and would, presumably, have been carried had not the Great Central itself changed its mind in favour of a lifting bridge just a few yards north of the existing alignment. This could be done without Parliamentary powers because the new work was within the deviation limits allowed under the 1861 Act. Local authorities contributed to the cost because a road deck was incorporated on the bridge alongside the double track railway. The latter was rebuilt on a new alignment most of the way from Keadby Junction to Gunhouse Junction but the earlier idea of a new route all the way to Frodingham was dropped. Instead, part of the long viaduct was filled in to make an embankment. A new station was provided at Althorpe but there was no need to replace Gunness as there was pedestrian access over the bridge to Althorpe. The complete works were opened on 21 May 1916.

The bridge comprised five spans: from the east, there was an approach span of 70ft, then one of 40ft upon which the lifting span rolled. This was 160 ft in length and was followed by two fixed river spans of 135 ft each. It was electrically operated but, with no mains supply in the area, it had to have its own generating plant. It became a fixed bridge in 1960, when BR were authorised to remove the lifting mechanism because there were no longer any ships with high masts or funnels.

Train services

Historically, the passenger service was nothing like today's regular interval pattern. Taking 1910 as an example, the first eastbound departure from Crowle was at 7.02am for all stations to Cleethorpes (non stop between Habrough and Grimsby Town). Next was the 9.15 all stations (without exception) to Cleethorpes. Then at 9.45 came the express from Leeds Central to Cleethorpes calling at Frodingham & Scunthorpe, Grimsby Town, Grimsby Docks and New Clee (a station which has definitely declined in importance).This train also stopped at Habrough by request to set down passengers from Wakefield or beyond. The next train at 10.54 am had a conditional stop at Althorpe to set down from Doncaster or beyond. It then called at Frodingham and Barnetby,

where it stood for 18 minutes before proceeding all stations to Cleethorpes, having amalgamated with a train from Manchester. Except on Thursdays when it left Barnetby six minutes ahead of the train from Manchester and ran non-stop to Grimsby Town, then Docks, New Clee and Cleethorpes. The significance of Thursday was Brigg market day, when both trains would convey additional carriages. That was the entire morning service. The next eastbound train from Crowle was at 12.41 semi fast to Cleethorpes. There weren't any expresses missing Crowle, nor were there any locals starting from Frodingham - at least not in a morning. There was a 1.30pm all stations to Cleethorpes starting from Frodingham upon which the stop at Elsham was by request.

If we move forward half a century to 1960, the timetable is a lot worse. There is a mail and passenger train, through from Manchester Piccadilly via Penistone and Barnsley. This leaves Doncaster at 3.17am, stands for 15 minutes at Scunthorpe & Frodingham, then calls at Barnetby, Grimsby Town (16 minute layover), Grimsby Docks and Cleethorpes. If you weren't up that early, there are only two other morning trains eastbound. The 5.49 from Doncaster calls at all stations except New Clee and takes 2 hours 40 minutes to reach Cleethorpes. It is timed to stand between three and eight minutes at Stainforth & Hatfield, Thorne South, Althorpe, Scunthorpe, Barnetby, Grimsby Town and Grimsby Docks. These allowances will have been for unloading mail and parcels and may have been dictated by the Post Office. So, if we're looking for something like a respectable passenger train, it will have to be 9.09 DMU from Doncaster, all stations to Habrough, then Grimsby Town, Grimsby Docks and Cleethorpes, reached in 2 hours 2 minutes. That concludes the morning service. The next train is the 12.25 DMU, all stations from Doncaster to Cleethorpes except Barnby Dun, with Appleby (Lincs) and New Clee stops on Saturdays only.

Compared to all this, the present day service is both more frequent and simpler to explain: Hourly express Manchester Airport to Cleethorpes, hourly slow Sheffield to Scunthorpe.

WD No 90024 travelling west from Althorpe on 6 April 1964, passing one of the three position semaphores installed in 1916. The signal is at caution, the clear position was vertical. *(David Holmes)*

Class O4 2 – 8 – 0 No 63634 has come off the goods line at Brocklesby and is now heading for Grimsby *(A M Ross)*

WD 2 – 8 – 0 No 90425 entering Grimsby Town from the west with a stone train in Summer 1957. Horse boxes stand in the siding by Wellowgate box. Young trainspotters and a mail cart complete the scene. *(A M Ross)*

Doncaster based B1 No 61120 restarts from Grimsby Town with a stopper for Cleethorpes in Summer 1957. The East Lincs line branches off at Garden Street. *(A M Ross)*

37094 and 37055 pass the closed station at Appleby with iron ore from Immingham to Frodingham on 29 July 1979. *(Tom Heavyside)*

Steel production is now concentrated on the Appleby – Frodingham site to the south of the main line. *(Stuart Baker)*

Heavy diesel power at the British Steel (now Corus) loco shed *(Stuart Baker)*

It takes two of these locos, one on each end, to move a "torpedo" car, laden with molten steel.
(Stuart Baker)

This page The Appleby Frodingham Railway Preservation Society offers a tour round the Steel plant with a somewhat overbearing commentary. A 1912 Peckett 0 – 4 – 0ST waits to start from the Society`s Excursion Platform at the head of former DMU passenger stock.
(Martin Bairstow)

Part way through the tour there is a break at the Society`s depot, where refreshment can be had in the well appointed Lounge Car.
(Martin Bairstow)

Traffic on the internal system is controlled on a kind of permissive block system.
(Martin Bairstow)

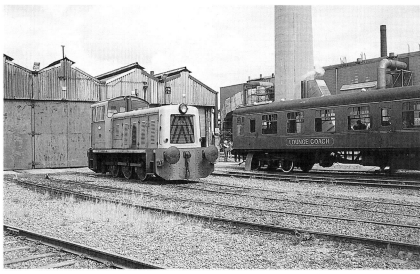

opposite page upper "Jurassic" at South Sea Lane on the Lincolnshire Coast Light Railway in 1984. The fireman is Jim Smith, mentioned on page 110.The carriages are two from the Ashover Light Railway and the sole passenger coach from Sand Hutton. *(John Holroyd)*

opposite page lower Vessels from the BR fleet used to go to Immingham for annual overhaul in the dry dock. The former Great Western steamer "St Patrick" is moored in the main dock in March 1967.
(Peter Sunderland)

The Barton & Immingham Light Railway

The title is a bit of a misnomer. The line didn't run from Barton and was a light railway only because it was authorised by an Order, made in 1907 under the Light Railways Act.

The main object was to provide a service between Hull and Immingham so a single line was built for 7 miles between Goxhill and Immingham West Junction where it made a triangular junction with the Humber Commercial Railway. It was opened for goods, between Killingholme and Immingham on 1 December 1910 and throughout on 1 May 1911 when a passenger service began between New Holland Pier and a station on the western jetty at Immingham Dock.

The Barton to Goxhill section was never built. It might have happened had the North Lindsey Light Railway been extended from Winteringham to Barton, though there was always the alternative of doubling the existing Barton branch from New Holland in the quest for a route from Scunthorpe to Immingham via the banks of the Humber. The First World War put an end to such speculation.

The New Holland - Goxhill - Immingham route survived as a something of a backwater for 52 years. Steam gave way to diesel multiple units on 2 July 1956, with five workings each way Mondays to Fridays. There were two extra trains on Saturdays but none at all on Sundays. The passenger trains were withdrawn on 15 June 1963, when the line closed completely between Goxhill and Killingholme. It is still open for goods southwards from Killingholme.

A Class 114 DMU has arrived at Immingham Dock on 27 June 1959. Introduced in 1956, these units were known as "Derby Heavyweights" or "Lincolnshire" sets as the majority spent their working lives in the area. The 50 motor coaches were numbered 50000 to 50049 and the trailers 56000 to 56049. Later these numbers were changed to 530xx and 540xx to avoid confusion with class 50 and class 56 diesel locos. They had all been withdrawn by 1992 but two sets are preserved at Butterley. *(John Oxley)*

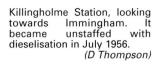

Killingholme Station, looking towards Immingham. It became unstaffed with dieselisation in July 1956.
(D Thompson)

A "Derby Heavyweight" (later class 114) DMU approaching Goxhill on a run from Immingham to New Holland on 24 June 1961.
(John Oxley)

East Halton looking towards Goxhill. This too was unstaffed from July 1956
(Alan Young Collection)

A class 114 DMU on a special at Admiralty Platform on 7 October 1967. *(RCTS)*

The same special at Immingham Dock Station.
(RCTS)

Class D7 4 - 4 – 0 No 5683 at Immingham in 1934 with a train of six wheelers for New Holland.
(Chris Bates collection)

Class B1 No 61056 calls at Grimsby Docks with the Saturday lunchtime workmen`s train from Immingham to Cleethorpes on 29 December 1962.
(Roger Hockney)

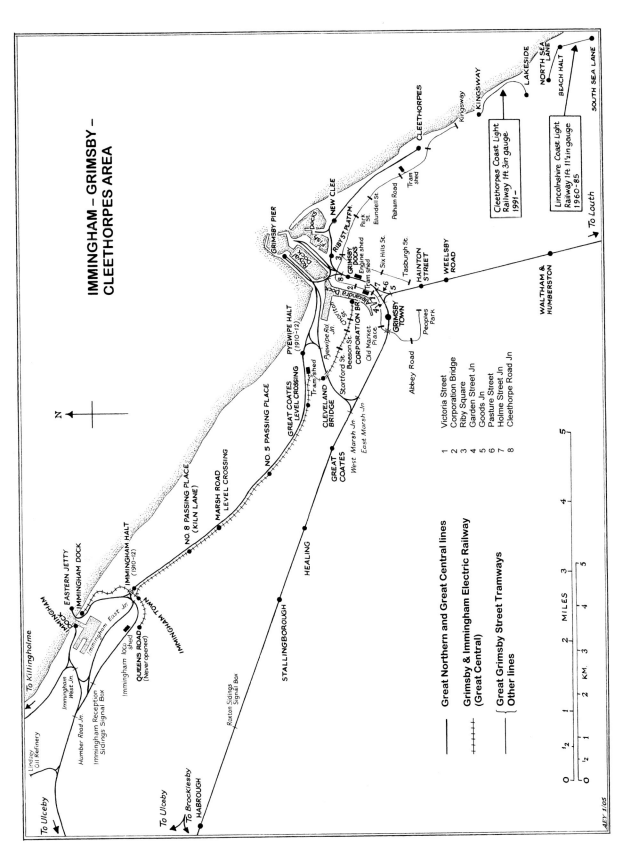

IMMINGHAM – GRIMSBY – CLEETHORPES AREA

Cleethorpes Coast Light Railway 1ft 3in gauge 1991 –

Lincolnshire Coast Light Railway 1ft 11½in gauge 1960–85

Key points:

1	Victoria Street
2	Corporation Bridge
3	Riby Square
4	Garden Street Jn
5	Goods Jn
6	Pasture Street
7	Holme Street Jn
8	Cleethorpe Road Jn

Great Northern and Great Central lines

Grimsby & Immingham Electric Railway (Great Central)

Great Grimsby Street Tramways

Other lines

Locations (selected):

To Killingholme, To Ulceby, To Brocklesby, HABROUGH, To Ulceby, To Louth

Lindsey Oil Refinery, IMMINGHAM DOCK, EASTERN JETTY, Immingham West Jn, Humber Road Jn, Immingham Reception Sidings Signal Box, Immingham Loco shed, IMMINGHAM TOWN, QUEENS ROAD (Never opened), Roxton Sidings Signal Box, Immingham East Jn, IMMINGHAM HALT (1910–12), No.8 PASSING PLACE (KILN LANE), MARSH ROAD LEVEL CROSSING, No.5 PASSING PLACE, STALLINGBOROUGH, HEALING, GREAT COATES, GREAT COATES LEVEL CROSSING, PYEWIPE HALT (1910–12), CLEVELAND BRIDGE, Tram shed, West Marsh Jn, East Marsh Jn, CORPORATION BRIDGE, Pyewipe Rd Jn, Stortford St., Beeson St., Old Market Place, Cross St., Alexandra Dock, Scartho St., Abbey Road, Peoples Park, GRIMSBY TOWN, HAINTON STREET, Engine shed, Tram shed, GRIMSBY DOCKS, RIBY ST PLATFM, Park St., Blundell St., Six Hills St., Tasburgh St., Pelham Road, Tram shed, WEELSBY ROAD, WALTHAM & HUMBERSTON, Docks, GRIMSBY PIER, NEW CLEE, CLEETHORPES, Kingsway, KINGSWAY, LAKESIDE, NORTH SEA LANE, BEACH HALT, SOUTH SEA LANE

N

AEY 1/05

MILES 0 ½ 1 2 3 4 5

KM 0 1 2 3 4 5

The Grimsby District Light Railway

No 14 at Corporation Bridge on 25 September 1955. The Parcels Office will have been a collection point for all railway parcels, not just for the tram.

(J C W Halliday)

The direct rail link from Grimsby to Immingham took the form of a goods line, alongside which was laid an electric tramway. The goods line was twice increased from single to double track and twice reduced back again. It is still open, albeit now with only sparse traffic.

Rather than seek a private Act, the Great Central invoked the simplified procedure in the Light Railways Act, 1896. An Order was granted in January 1906 for a line from Corporation Bridge, Grimsby, which would begin by a triangular junction off the Great Grimsby Street Tramways. The line was to connect at Pyewipe with the existing Great Coates branch, itself being remodelled in connection with the Immingham venture.

As the priority was to move construction materials to Immingham, the section beyond Pyewipe was the first to be built. From May 1906 until late 1909, the single line was used by the contractors. Then it was handed over to the Great Central who introduced a limited passenger service from 3 January 1910.

Wooden stations were erected at Pyewipe Road and at Immingham to accommodate a steam rail motor, which made four return trips each weekday. The passenger service made no connection with any other railway. It only ran until May 1912, when it was superseded by the adjacent electric tramway. The original light railway then continued as a goods line. The track was doubled in 1914 but reduced back to single just three years later. The second track was requisitioned by the Government, probably for use in sidings at munitions factories. Although the Railway will have been compensated, replacement of the second track did not begin until 1948, when extra capacity was needed for the new petro chemical industries being developed on the Humber Bank. Double track working was finally reintroduced on 17 September 1951.

Traffic has since fallen off and the line was singled again in 1984. The loss of rail traffic from Novartis (formerly Ciba Geigy) and Acordis (formerly Courtaulds) has left the Grimsby District Light Railway with very little traffic.

The Electric Line

Taking up the powers in the 1906 Light Railway Order, the Great Central laid a single track in the road from Corporation Bridge to Pyewipe, and then an additional track alongside the Grimsby District Light Railway to a station at Immingham Town. Electric power was supplied by the Company's own power plant at Immingham. After 1957, it came from the National Grid.

There were three passing loops on the street section and a further eight on the Light Railway proper, though four of these were removed in 1917. The line opened on 15 May 1912, with a basic half hourly service, greatly enhanced at peak times. There was no signalling. Single line security relied on strict observance of the working timetable.

There were several intermediate stops, some compulsory and some by request. It was possible to book tickets to places rejoicing in names such as No 5 Passing Place and No 8 Passing Place.

A proposed connection with the Great Grimsby Street Tramways was never built. It would have required strengthening of the Corporation Bridge over Alexandra Dock. This was not achieved until 1928, by which time the municipal tramway was already in terminal decline.

The tramway was extended at the other end on 17 November 1913. From this date, trams arriving at Immingham Town from Grimsby reversed direction to continue on double track to a new terminus by the eastern jetty at Immingham Dock separated from the "main line" station by the lock at the dock entrance.

An extension, less than ¾ mile in length was built from Immingham Town to Queens Road, just short of the Immingham Loco Shed. It was inspected by the Board of Trade on 20 July 1915 and approved for opening but, despite local protest, it was never brought into use. The Queens Road extension would have saved a walk for the many Immingham loco crews who travelled to work from Grimsby, often in the early hours of the morning.

16 single deck bogie tramcars were supplied by Brush between 1911 and 1915. Nos 1 to 4 and 9 to 16 were the long 64 seat vehicles, which were always the mainstay of the service. They were the longest tramcars ever to run in this Country, not counting recent articulated vehicles. They were pretty uncomfortable, with reversible wooden seats.

Nos 5 to 8 were shorter 40 seat vehicles intended for the through running into Grimsby town centre, which never happened. They saw some use on local workings between Corporation Bridge and Cleveland Bridge but were withdrawn in the 1930s when the short workings were abolished. No 5 survived as the permanent way vehicle. By the late 1940s, additional capacity was required to accommodate traffic to new factories alongside the Humber Estuary. Three trams were bought from Newcastle in 1948 and given the vacant numbers 6 to 8. They were not a success. 18 more were bought from the Gateshead & District Tramways in 1951.

Decline and Closure

The demise of the Grimsby & Immingham was not for want of patronage. The line would have met the test of 10,000 passengers a week, set by the Beeching Report in 1963. It was in need of complete renewal, the cost of which was never contemplated. Around 1955, BR did consider adapting the adjacent Light Railway to carry a DMU service, accessing Grimsby Town Station via West Marsh Junction. Nothing came of this idea, which would have been consistent with the desire of Grimsby Corporation to

No 16 waits at No 5 Passing Place alongside the double track Grimsby District Light Railway in September 1959.   *(Peter Sunderland)*

No 12 at the out of town Cleveland Bridge terminus on 27 June 1959. Here the dwindling number of passengers had to change onto bus or bicycle.

(John Oxley)

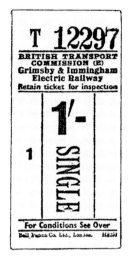

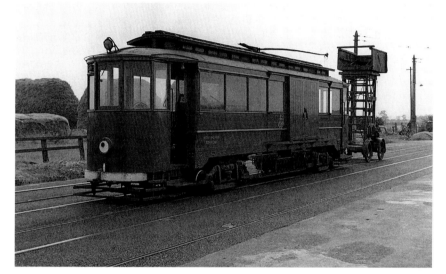

No 34, ex Gateshead, was renumbered in the BR engineering fleet when it became the permanent way car. DE 320224 on the double track street section between Immingham Town and Dock in September 1955.

(J C W Halliday)

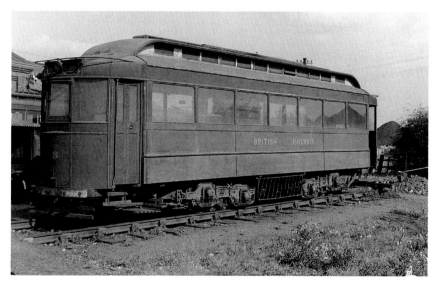

The second No 8, ex Newcastle, looking forlorn at Pyewipe Depot in September 1955. *(J C W Halliday)*

be rid of the 1¼ mile street section.

In 1948/9, the Corporation had pressed for closure of this stretch but would not meet the costs demanded by BR. Instead, BR relaid some of the track and the Corporation put a tarmac surface over the setts in the roadway. In 1955, the Corporation threatened to invoke its power of compulsory purchase under the original Light Railway Order. This, in itself, could not force closure but BR responded with an offer to give the line to the Corporation if the latter paid the cost of demolition and put on a replacement bus service.

There was a delay whilst the matter passed through the consultative procedure but on 30 June 1956, the street section was closed. The remainder of the tramway continued operating as before with a basic half hourly service from early morning until late evening, with extras at peak times and a limited number of departures right through the night. A Corporation bus ran in connection, though many workers found it more convenient to leave their bicycles at Cleveland Bridge, which became a major park and ride station (for cyclists).

Banished to an out of town terminus, the line lost some traffic but was still important to many workers as there was no adequate road to Immingham. In 1958, BR invoked the consultation process, seeking complete closure of the tramway. In support of

closure, they cited high staffing costs, due to the inability to run trams in multiple. Some timetabled journeys actually involved up to seven independent trams. BR also claimed low earnings due to one third of the passengers having free passes, though after closure they had to pay bus fares for a lot of the people concerned.

The Report of the Transport Users Consultative Committee remarked that they were used to dealing with closures affecting tens or even hundreds of passengers but here was a case involving thousands. They were persuaded that the roads were inadequate to convey all the passengers by bus. A compromise was agreed so, from 28 September 1959, trams ran only in the morning and evening peaks on Mondays to Fridays, and at the morning peak and lunchtime on Saturdays. The restricted service did not appear in "Bradshaw" and through tickets were no longer available from main line stations. The arrangement was to last a maximum of two years. In the event, final closure was fixed for Saturday 1 July 1961.

Three trams are preserved. Nos 14 and 20 (Gateshead No 5) are at the National Tramway Museum at Crich whilst 26 (Gateshead 10) conveys visitors around the North of England open air museum at Beamish in County Durham.

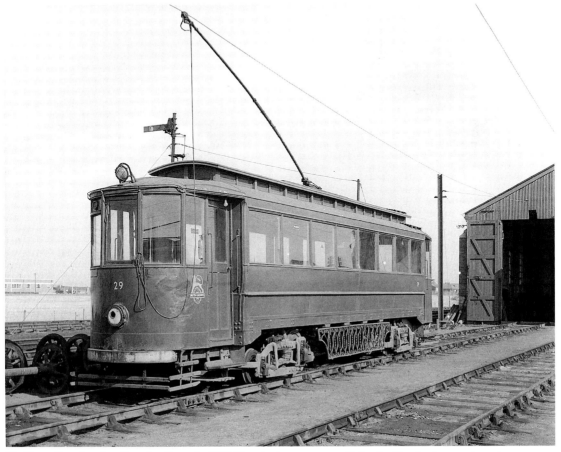

No 29, ex Gateshead, at Pyewipe Depot in 1955. The shed was very small, the fleet having to spend most of its life out of doors.   (J C W Halliday)

A steam railcar at the temporary Immingham Halt which was only open from 3 January 1910 until 14 May 1912. The Great Central had three steam railcars dating from 1903/4. One had worked between New Holland and Barton.
(Martin Bairstow Collection)

Pyewipe Shed Yard, September 1959 with ex Gateshead No 24 closest to the camera. The goods line is on the left, the tramway to Cleveland Bridge to the right.
(Peter Sunderland)

No 12 has left the railway alignment and is climbing up towards Immingham Town, September 1959.
(Peter Sunderland)

The Great Grimsby Street Tramways Company

Old Market Place, Grimsby.

Tram No 9 leaving the Old Market Place, near Grimsby Town Station, for People's Park after it had gained a top cover about 1909. The Cleethorpes bound track took the left turn into Victoria Street, rejoining the incoming track after ¼ mile.
(Martin Bairstow Collection)

This enterprise began as a horse tramway in 1881, switching to electric power in 1901. The system survived until 1937 but was at its maximum extent of 6¼ route miles only for a period of 20 years from 1906. The "main line" ran from Peoples Park in Grimsby to Kingsway in Cleethorpes. The track was standard gauge, laid in the street, and was double apart from the initial section from Peoples Park to the Old Market Place. A branch, single track with passing loops, ran due south from Riby Square to Tasburgh Street but was never extended the short distance to make end on connection with the "main line" at Peoples Park. Statutory powers existed but no agreement was reached with the Great Northern Railway to lay track over the level crossing at Hainton Street.

The horse drawn service began on 4 June 1881, over three miles of single track between Bargate and Park Street, plus the branch to Tasburgh Street. Seven double deck trams were used, each seating 32 passengers, 16 inside and 16 on the exposed upper deck. They were housed in a depot at Park Street. A single horse was employed except on the slight gradient over the railway bridge near Grimsby Town. Here a stable lad had to be on hand with a second horse, just for the short incline on the otherwise level route. The same thing also happened, after 1898, on Isaacs Hill, Cleethorpes where the second horse had to be detached without stopping the tram once the summit had been reached.

They didn't bother too much with animal welfare, nor were employee conditions that wonderful. Hours were longer and wages lower than would have applied either on the Great Central Railway or with Grimsby Corporation. The latter body seems to have had this in mind when the time came for electrification.

Under the Tramways Act, 1870, the Corporation had powers of compulsory purchase after 21 years,

that is in 1902. Some authorities would have negotiated this forward in order to carry out electrification themselves. But Grimsby and neighbouring Cleethorpes agreed, for a price, to defer their powers until 21 years after electrification. This, they claimed, would give a better deal for the ratepayers because the Tramways Company could operate more cheaply than they would and could thus afford to pay the wayleave which they had negotiated.

The Great Grimsby Street Tramways Company was always a subsidiary of the Provincial Tramways Group, whose Empire in the electric era comprised this line plus Portsdown & Horndean, Gosport & Fareham and the Plymouth, Stonehouse & Devonport Light Railways. The Group had been forced to sell its larger Portsmouth and Cardiff systems to the respective Corporations, and had been able to finance the Grimsby electrification out of the proceeds.

31 four wheel double deck electric trams were acquired between 1901 and 1906. In common with most systems, these began with open tops but most of them soon received balcony covers. Until 1918, six double deck former horse trams were available to be hauled as trailers at busy periods.

The electric tram depot and generating plant were at Pelham Road, Cleethorpes. This was close to the Great Central Railway, from which a siding was laid for coal and other deliveries. The power plant supplied the tramway within Cleethorpes. It also sold electricity to the Council for street lighting. Beyond Park Street, it was the other way round with the Tramway buying electricity from Grimsby Corporation.

A single deck tram, No 38, was purchased from Southport in 1915. The only other single decker, No 40 was built in 1922. Looking like a charabanc on rails, it ran for three seasons as a "Special Touring

Car" between Kingsway and Peoples Park. In 1925, it was sold to the Portsdown & Horndean Light Railway.

Traffic reached a peak in 1921, by which time both track and rolling stock was overdue for some heavy expenditure. This the Company was unwilling to meet, in view of its uncertain tenure. Grimsby Corporation decided in favour of municipal ownership and promoted a Parliamentary Bill, which was passed in August 1921. Vesting day for the tramway in Grimsby, but not Cleethorpes, was to be 21 July 1922 but it took until 6 April 1925 to settle the deal by arbitration

On this latter date, ownership of the small system was divided at Park Street. The Company retained the line in Cleethorpes, including Pelham Road depot. This continued to house the entire fleet until 1 January 1927, when the vehicles allocated to Grimsby were removed to a new facilty in Victoria Street, Grimsby, near Corporation Bridge. The building here was a First World War seaplane hanger, transported from Killingholme. Separate ownership did not prevent through working of trams between Grimsby and Cleethorpes.

The purpose of the Corporation take over had been to renew the tramway, not to close it. But even in the time consumed by the arbitration, circumstances were changing rapidly. In particular, the trolley bus seemed to offer a let out from the cost of tramway renewal.

By 1925, the rolling stock was at the end of its life. Grimsby Corporation bought 16 second hand trams from Sunderland, but closed the branch to Tasburgh Street on 2 October 1926. The section from Old Market Place to Peoples Park followed on 2 June 1928.

Between 1925 and 1928, the Tramways Company built eight new trams at its Cleethorpes Works. In 1929 it bought 12 open top cars from Gosport & Fareham, some of which it fitted with balcony top covers. Both Company and Corporation put off major track renewal until they reached the point

No 22 at Kingsway terminus in Cleethorpes in June 1933. Built for the Gosport & Fareham Tramway in 1905, it never acquired a top cover. *(Martin Bairstow Collection)*

where the tramway was just hanging on, waiting to be superseded. The Grimsby Corporation section all but closed on 21 November 1936 except that some Cleethorpes trams continued to start from Riby Square until the following 31 March when the line was further cut back to Park Street.

During 1935, the Company had agreed to sell its remaining section to Cleethorpes Council. Vesting day was 15 July 1936 but the only purpose of the move was closure of the remaining tramway, which took place on 17 July 1937. Apart from Peoples Park, the entire system was replaced by trolley buses.

The original No 24, of 1901, at Kingsway terminus.
(Martin Bairstow Collection)

Grimsby for the Continent

The 1,631 ton "Dewsbury" served the Great Central and its successors from 1910 until 1959.
(Peter Sunderland collection)

Like other Railway Companies, the MS&L needed specific Parliamentary powers before it could operate steamships. Yet there never seemed to be any problem if a Railway got round the law by taking a slightly indirect route into the shipping business.

In May 1852, the MS&L gave financial support to the North of Europe Steamship Company to open a weekly service between Grimsby and Hamburg. Three years later, the MS&L and the still independent South Yorkshire Railway joined with French interests to promote the Anglo French Steamship Company. By July 1856, this enterprise had three ships operating between Grimsby and the Continent. This upset the North of Europe Company, which pulled out of Grimsby, leaving the Anglo French to expand its fleet and take on the Hamburg route.

None of which could hold back the Railway's ambition to have its own fleet. Having seen its Parliamentary Bill rejected in 1855, the Company was more successful in 1864. Powers to serve French Ports were denied but, otherwise, the Company's vessels could sail from Grimsby to most points from Antwerp to the Baltic. Three paddle and five screw steamers were taken over from the Anglo French Company and twice weekly routes were established to Hamburg and Rotterdam.

The fleet was renewed completely during the 1880s with eight new ships bearing the names of towns served by the Railway: "Gainsborough", "Retford", "Lincoln", "Chester", "Ashton", "Northenden", "Warrington" and "Oldham". This naming policy continued throughout the Company's life. Four vessels ordered in 1890 reflected the drive south towards London: "Nottingham", "Staveley", "Lutterworth" and "Leicester". Later names reflected the Company's claim on certain towns, which could only be justified by running powers over other railways.

Sailings to Scandinavia were provided by Wilson Line and DFDS. On 27 August 1889, Thomas Wilson, Sons & Company began a weekly service to Copenhagen and Malmo. Less than a year later, it was the turn of Det Forenede Dampskibs Selskab, (The United Steamship Company) to open its service to Grimsby when the "Fano" arrived from Esbjerg on 15 June 1890. The weekly service for passengers and general cargo was increased to twice weekly in 1894.

The 1910 timetable shows the Great Central service at its full extent. Ships for all destinations left Grimsby early evening, as soon as passengers and luggage had been transferred from the "boat trains", which ran daily except Sundays.

A "Through Express" left Leeds Central at 4.08pm stopping at Holbeck, Wakefield Westgate, Stainforth & Hatfield, Crowle, Frodingham and Grimsby Town to arrive Grimsby Docks at 6.16pm, whence it continued to Cleethorpes. The "Continental Boat Express" left Liverpool Central at 2.30pm and Manchester Central at 3.20 with portions for both Cleethorpes and Harwich Parkeston Quay. The latter parted company at Sheffield Victoria, whence the Cleethorpes train proceeded to Worksop, Retford, Gainsborough, Brigg, Grimsby Town and Grimsby Docks, arrive 6.45pm. The timetable implies that the Cleethorpes train dropped one or more carriages at Grimsby Docks Station to be shunted onto the quayside.

During May to September, on Tuesdays, Thursdays and Saturdays only, the Rotterdam sailing days, a "Restaurant Corridor Express" left Liverpool Central at 3.30pm and, with stops at Manchester, Sheffield and Retford, arrived "alongside the steamer" at 7.17pm.

Railway owned vessels sailed six days a week for Hamburg, taking 30 hours. Antwerp was served on Mondays, Wednesdays and Saturdays in 20 hours and Rotterdam on Tuesdays, Thursdays and Saturdays. Connecting with the same trains, Wilson Line left for Malmo on Tuesdays and Gothenburg on

The "Somerset" leaving Grimsby for Esbjerg in July 1967.   (Peter Sunderland)

Saturdays whilst DFDS sailed for Esbjerg on Mondays and Thursdays.

When there was no train "alongside the steamer", passengers and their luggage were carried to and from Grimsby Docks Station, free of charge, at least for the Railway Company steamers. It is unclear whether this applied also to Wilson Line and DFDS vessels.

Crossing time to Rotterdam in 1910 was 11 hours by the "magnificent" new 18 knot turbine steamers "Marylebone" and "Immingham". Launched in 1907, these had reduced the sailing time by a third but were not a commercial success. The accelerated timing did not justify the cost so, in 1911, they were re equipped with slower engines, single instead of triple propellers, one funnel instead of two and a service speed of 13 knots.

The last ships built for the Great Central were the quartet "Dewsbury", "Accrington", "Bury" and "Stockport", which emerged from Earle's of Hull in 1910/11. "Stockport" was a hastily ordered replacement for "Blackburn" which had suffered a collision on its maiden voyage, from Grimsby to Antwerp on 8 December 1910. Fortunately, it took five hours to sink allowing all on board to be rescued.

"Bury" was in Hamburg when the First World War broke out. It was seized by Germany and its crew interned. The same fate befell two older Great Central steamers "City of Leeds" and "City of Bradford", which were in German waters without the facility of a Marconi radio so they had no warning. All three came back in 1918. During the War, "Dewsbury" continued an irregular link with neutral Holland, but otherwise services were suspended. Four vessels were lost in the War: "Lincoln", "Leicester", "Wrexham" and "Immingham".

Passenger sailings resumed after 1919, but not on the same scale. Under the LNER, there was no incentive for Grimsby to compete with Hull and Harwich.

In 1935, the LNER ships at Grimsby and Hull were placed in joint management with those of the LMS at Goole under the name of Associated Humber Lines. Grimsby lost the Rotterdam passenger service but sailings to Hamburg continued, with a weekly departure from Grimsby on Saturdays at 7pm. On the fresh outbreak of war in 1939, "Bury" was in Grimsby, having left Hamburg for the last time on 24 August." The route never reopened.

"Stockport" was sunk in 1943, with massive loss of life, but the other three 1910/11 sisters resumed service with Associated Humber Lines after the War. "Dewsbury" left Antwerp for Hull on 31 January 1959, the final crossing by the last ex Great Central steamship.

During the Inter War period, DFDS carried passengers on its twice weekly Grimsby to Esbjerg run but the most important traffic was in Danish bacon and butter. It was this trade, which eventually took Grimsby into the roll on - roll off era with the opening of new port facilities on 18 January 1967. Instead of discharging produce wrapped in hessian, the new vessels "Somerset" and "Stafford" carried refrigerated trailers, which could be driven by road direct to the shops. This was bad news for rail freight but it did mark an important development both for the former Great Central port and for the Railway's one time Danish associate, DFDS. The success of the venture led to the commissioning in 1978 of larger ships, "Dana Cimbria" and "Dana Maxima". The latter was deliberately named to indicate its relation to the size of the entrance lock at Grimsby. There was no scope for expansion beyond this and DFDS left Grimsby for the last time on 28 May 1995, moving only as far as Immingham

"Suffolk" in the Royal Dock at Grimsby, May 1969. This vessel was smaller than the "Somerset" and "Stafford" and was more usually employed between Felixtowe and Copenhagen.
(Peter Sunderland)

The Port of Immingham

In terms of sheer tonnage, Immingham, once the Great Central's notorious white elephant, now holds the biggest promise of future traffic development.
Modern Railways (February 1966)

Perhaps "foresight" would have been better term than "white elephant". Today, Immingham is the busiest port in the Country and it is all thanks to the Great Central Railway.

A hundred years ago, both the volume of trade and the size of ships were growing beyond the capacity of Grimsby. In 1901, powers were obtained for a new dock at Grimsby but the Great Central hesitated before sinking money into the scheme. The Company was persuaded that no amount of dredging could keep open a channel at low tide for the size and draught of ship expected in the future.

By contrast, six miles upstream, the main channel of the Humber came close to the shore on the Lincolnshire side. The Railway had considered a port at Immingham as far back as 1874. In 1903, they decided to go for it. At first, Grimsby Corporation and other interests were opposed but, after making their own investigations, they began to support the scheme. Parliamentary powers were sought in 1903, but the Bill was dropped when clauses were inserted holding the Great Central liable for any silting of the Humber which, in the opinion of the Board of Trade, might be due to the development of Immingham. This was an unquantifiable liability, which the Great Central dare not assume.

Before resubmitting the Bill, the Great Central persuaded the Board of Trade that there was no threat to navigation in the Humber. The offending clauses were not reintroduced allowing the Humber Commercial Railway & Dock Act to pass on 22 July 1904. Work started in 1906, employing up to 2,500 men. One of the first tasks was to lay the Grimsby District Light Railway, which was available from May that year for the movement of men and materials.

The biggest feature of the Immingham development was the enclosed dock, which covers 45 acres. The central basin is 1,100 ft square, with two arms each 1,250 ft by 375 ft. The entrance lock is 840 ft by 90ft with three pairs of hydraulic gates. Immediately outside the entrance lock, two jetties curve out into the estuary. The south quay was the coal dock. Imported timber was handled in the north arm of the dock by five travelling steam cranes. Accessed from the main dock, was the graving dock, 740 ft by 56 ft, which ran parallel to the entrance lock. This was operated by a Great Central subsidiary, the Humber Graving Dock & Engineering Co, which overhauled the Railway steamers as well as outside commercial work.

Near to the Western Jetty was the power station, which supplied electricity to the whole complex as well as to the tramway to Grimsby. The Western Jetty was used for bunkering ships, which could take on coal without coming into the dock itself. Two rail tracks went out at right angles from a point near the Dock passenger station.

Altogether, some 170 miles of track were laid, including sidings. There were three railway routes into Immingham. Having been used by the contractor for four years, the Grimsby District Light Railway was handed over to the Great Central in 1910. The main line into Immingham was the Humber Commercial Railway, authorised by the same Act as the Dock itself. Opened on 3 January 1910, it ran for 3½ miles from Ulceby to Humber Road Junction, where it divided, one branch going to the Western Jetty, the other encircling the Dock to join the Grimsby District Light Railway, eventually reaching the Eastern Jetty. The third route was the strangely named Barton & Immingham Light Railway, which came from Goxhill to join the Humber Commercial Railway at Immingham West Junction.

The "Dewsbury" coaling at Immingham. Grimsby remained the Great Central passenger port.
(Garry Crossland collection)

In addition to works in the vicinity of Immingham, the scheme required 3½ miles of new railway near Doncaster. Anticipating significant coal and other freight between South Yorkshire and Immingham, the Great Central could not hope to route this through Doncaster Station. In 1903, it obtained powers for the Doncaster Avoiding Line, between Hexthorpe and Bentley Junctions. This passes over the Great Northern (the East Coast Main Line) north of Doncaster Station to join the Scunthorpe line by a flying junction. Work did not begin until 1908, allowing the link to open on 25 July 1910. Another project associated with Immingham was quadrupling the main line between Wrawby Junction and Brocklesby.

Not until the 1950s, was there a regular passenger service on the Humber Commercial Railway. The Eastern Jetty had a passenger berth and railway station. But, if it was ever intended that Great Central, Wilson Line or DFDS steamers would transfer to Immingham, then this never happened. The regular boat train connections remained at Grimsby until their demise. In Summer, during the 1920s and 30s, special trains did run out onto the Eastern Jetty at Immingham in connection with cruise ships to Scandinavia.

There was a passenger station near the Western Jetty, served by trains from New Holland over the Barton & Immingham Light Railway. From the early 1950s, this station also received a very sparse workmen's service by the Humber Commercial Railway, through from Cleethorpes. These trains, two inbound early morning and one return late afternoon (lunch time on Saturdays) were not advertised in the public timetable until June 1963 when they suddenly appeared on closure of the Barton & Immingham Light Railway. They were withdrawn in October 1969, since when Immingham has had no passenger trains.

It was for the export of coal that the investment in Immingham was best justified. The 2,350 ft long south quay was the coal dock with seven hydraulic hoists, each fed by eight sidings. There was storage space for 17,000 wagons.

The 1966 quote at the head of this chapter came at a time when BR and the Coal Board were contemplating new handling equipment to move export coal for Italy on the same "merry go round" principle which was then being introduced between colliery and power station.

Since the 1980s, the flow of coal has reversed. The south quay has been transformed into the Nordic Terminal, opened in 1995 for the roll on - roll off ferries of DFDS. Coal imports are now handled at the Humber International Terminal, which was commissioned in June 2000, out in the River, north west of the dock. Some 24 coal trains a day now leave Immingham with the number set to rise following closure, in Autumn 2004, of the Selby Coalfield.

Almost all the BR freight operation was privatised in 1996 to English Welsh & Scottish Railway, 22% of whose business is in traffic passing through

Shipping movements through the lock gate were controlled by semaphore signals, larger but otherwise similar to those used on the Railway. April 1960.
(Peter Sunderland)

Immingham. There is a modest amount of competition in the rail freight industry, with Freightliner also having a stake in the Immingham coal traffic. This means that Immingham accounts for between a fifth and a quarter of freight on the entire British network.

Besides coal, EWS traffic includes huge flows of iron ore to Scunthorpe. Crude oil comes from Welton, just south of Langworth on the Market Rasen line, for processing at Lindsey Oil Refinery, to which white spirit is moved in trip freights from Immingham. Acid is carried to Barry Docks, loaded billets of steel to Walsall. Steel comes back from there in winter heading for Toronto. There is finished steel slab from Avesta at Sheffield, scrap for export, newsprint from Northern Europe for Knowsley, Selby, Shotton and Scotland and DFDS containers known as "Mafis" transhipped into Ferrywagons leased from German Railways. A new traffic, which started in February 2004, is in imported boxed goods for IKEA distribution centres at Kettering, Peterborough and Doncaster. Another new flow, beginning in 2005, is in Bitumen from Lindsey Oil

"Tor Mercia" in the graving
dock at Immingham,
November 1969
(Peter Sunderland)

The DFDS Nordic Terminal ,
which stands on the south
quay, once dominated by coal
hoists. *(Martin Bairstow)*

Inside the Nordic terminal
where DFDS cargos are
transhipped to and from rail
wagons. *(Chris Bates)*

Refinery to the Total Fina terminal on Preston Docks, which is served by the Ribble Steam Railway. And so the list goes on: chemicals to Stalybridge, methanol to Lindsey Oil Refinery, zinc to Bloxwich, aluminium blocks to Bridgend, box and coil steel to Wolverhampton.

Tor Line

Immingham finally became a passenger port in April 1966, when the "Tor Anglia" opened a new era in North Sea shipping, offering a multi purpose roll on - roll off service on a triangular route between Immingham, Amsterdam and Gothenburg. Once the sister ship "Tor Hollandia" was also available, Immingham could offer one departure a week to Amsterdam and three to Gothenburg. Most traffic was car and lorry based but rail passengers were provided with a special bus from Grimsby Town. There was also a bus from Habrough Station on a Sunday when the connection from Doncaster was too tight to go via Grimsby.

After ten years, the pioneer ships were sold to the Mediterranean, where they were still in service in 2004. Their replacements were the larger "Tor Britannia" and "Tor Scandinavia", which could just fit through the entrance lock at Immingham.

The new ships were not at Immingham for long. In 1977, the passenger operation was transferred to Felixtowe, leaving Immingham with the roll on - roll off freight ferries, which had developed alongside the multi purpose vessels.

Tor Line became part of the Danish Group DFDS in 1981. Four years later, DFDS transferred their own longstanding Grimsby operation to Immingham. Today, the combined DFDS Tor Line is the largest

"Tor Magnolia" steaming past Spurn Head, one of six 32,400 sister ships to enter service with DFDS Tor Line between 2003 and 2005. *(DFDS)*

"Tor Anglia" arrives by Amsterdam Centraal Station on its inaugural run from Immingham in 1966. A young reporter, Chris Bates, was on board covering the story for the Grimsby "Sunday Link".

(Peter Sunderland collection)

shipping operator at Immingham, which is, in turn, the busiest port in the UK. Roll on - roll off vessels leave on seven days a week to Gothenburg, on six to Rotterdam and to Esbjerg, five to Cuxhaven and twice a week to Kristiansand and Bruvik in Norway. Much of the traffic is in road trailers but a significant amount is taken off the ships on special trucks straight into the DFDS Nordic terminal for loading onto rail. A limited number of passengers are carried on most sailings. In 2003, DFDS Tor Line took delivery of the 32,400 ton "Tor Minerva" the first of six sister ships to appear over the following two years. They are just able to negotiate the lock entrance to Immingham, but will soon transfer to the two new river berths upon which Associated British Ports began work in 2004.

The Port of Killingholme

Whilst Associated British Ports was planning its deep water roll on - roll off facility at Immingham, two river berths had already appeared at nearby Killingholme. On 24 October 2000, Stena Line began a roll on - roll off freight only service between Killingholme and the Hook of Holland. The two ship

service runs overnight, six days a week. New larger vessels are being built to replace the "Stena Searider" (1969) and "Stena Seatrader" (1973) with which the service was launched.

The Port of Killingholme is owned by Simon Group, which also owns Sutton Bridge in Norfolk. A rail link is advertised, courtesy of the truncated Barton & Immingham Light Railway. Roll on - roll off services are also run by Seawheel to Rotterdam and by Cobelfret to Hamburg, Esbjerg and Gothenburg.

Passengers to Immingham?

With so many people employed at Immingham, we may ask why has there been no passenger service there since 1969? Of course it would be inconvenient to superimpose a passenger timetable onto the freight operation and of course "everybody" owns a car, but these are arguments for not running passenger trains anywhere at all.

The Railway Industry is a joke, and ultimately doomed to failure, if it runs heavily subsidised trains to Thornton Abbey (12 passengers a day) and Kirton Lindsey (no passengers at all) yet ignores destinations to which people really do travel.

"Clementine" and "Melusine" at Immingham on 20 April 2004. Later that year, Cobelfret (Compagnie Belge d'Affretements) transferred its Zeebrugge and Rotterdam services from Immingham to Killingholme.

(Martin Bairstow)

153 307 calls at Thornton Abbey on 12 July 1996. Not a lot of traffic here.

(Stuart Baker)

Locomotives on Shed at 40B Immingham

By F W Smith

Opened in 1912 to coincide with inauguration of the extensive dock estate, Immingham was the last of the Great Central's large sheds to be brought into use. It closed to steam in 1966 but a new diesel repair and maintenance shed was built on the site. The derelict coaling tower still stands.

On my visit on Sunday 23 October 1955, there were no fewer than 121 locomotives on shed.

A5	4 - 6 - 2T	69803/ 13/ 20
B1	4 - 6 - 0	61079/ 82, 61130/ 42/ 44/ 59/ 68/ 95, 61248/ 84, 61318/ 74/ 79/ 90, 61406 /08
B16	4 - 6 - 0	61446
J6	0 - 6 - 0	64244
J11	0 - 6 - 0	64314/ 23/ 28/ 55/ 76/ 95, 64404/ 39/ 46
J39	0 - 6 - 0	64722, 64881, 64967
J63	0 - 6 - 0T	68204/ 05/ 07/ 10
J94	0 - 6 - 0ST	68009/ 18/ 20/ 22/ 26/ 28/ 33/ 67/ 68/ 69/ 71/ 72/ 73/ 74/ 75/ 76/ 77/ 78/ 80
K2	2 - 6 - 0	61725/ 27/ 36/ 46/ 78
K3	2 - 6 - 0	61802/ 03/ 06/ 36/ 39, 61950
N5	0 - 6 - 0T	69309
O2	2 - 8 - 0	63948
O4	2 - 8 - 0	63615/ 16/ 44/ 65/ 90/ 92, 63737/ 38/ 50/ 59/ 65, 63801/ 02/ 19/ 36/ 40/ 78/ 91 63900
WD	2 - 8 - 0	90003/ 35/ 52/ 87, 90118/ 31, 90211/21/ 23/ 24/ 55/ 59/ 76, 90431/ 53/ 77/ 92 90540/ 83, 90660, 90717
Diesel	0 - 6 - 0	11108, 12127/ 33/ 34, 13153/ 54/ 55/ 56/ 57/ 58/ 60/ 61

Seven of the above were stored: 61746, 61778, 64722, 64881, 68020, 68022, 69309

Immingham based K3 No 61950 approaching Brocklesby with fish from Grimsby to Banbury in 1957.   *(A M Ross)*

Class B1 No 61406 at Immingham Shed on 28 August 1965. This engine regularly worked the morning Cleethorpes – Leeds Central and teatime return.   *(RCTS)*

The North Lindsey Light Railway

The remoteness of Whitton terminus, alongside the Humber. At one time, the GC and L&Y Railways were prepared to fight over this territory. *(John Oxley)*

Promoted independently, this enterprise might have come to nothing had the Great Central not decided to support it. In part, the interest of the Great Central arose from a desire to stop the Lancashire & Yorkshire Railway from gaining a foothold east of the Trent.

A century later, it seems incredible that two main line companies would have been rivals for the rather unproductive territory on the south bank of the Humber between the Trent and Barton. In the event, the North Lindsey Light Railway was built. The northern reach never achieved much but the southern section became an integral part of the Scunthorpe steel industry.

The North Lindsey gained its Light Railway Order in January 1900. It did not aspire to be an operating company, but entered into a working agreement with the Great Central. The first six miles of single track opened on 3 September 1906 from just east of Frodingham Station to West Halton. The junction faced east so that a train from Frodingham would have had to reverse to gain access to the branch. To avoid this, the passenger service began at a small station, just on the branch, called Scunthorpe.

Passenger trains terminated at Winterton & Thealby. The station at West Halton was not opened until the line was extended to Winteringham on 15 July 1907. A service of three trains was then offered in each direction, excluding Sundays. At the same time, a short goods branch was opened to Winteringham Haven.

The Great Central was suspicious of Lancashire & Yorkshire Railway ambitions east of the Trent. In 1904, the L&Y had sought Parliamentary powers to run steamships between Goole and Hull, serving intermediate ports, including Winteringham Haven, where they hoped to build a jetty or even a dock. Opposed by the Great Central, the L&Y Bill passed

but only to run ships between Goole, Hull and the Continent - no intermediate calls in the Humber. The same year had seen an application before the Light Railway Commissioners for an Ackworth & Lindsey Light Railway. 54 miles including branches, this would have begun in L&Y territory, would have made a junction with the Axholme Joint, crossed the Trent, joined the North Lindsey at Winteringham and would then have continued to Barton, Goxhill and Immingham. The promoters had still to decide between a Trent bridge or tunnel, when the Light Railway Commissioners told them to seek full Parliamentary powers for a venture on such a scale.

In 1907, the L&Y itself deposited a Bill to extend the Fockerby branch of the Axholme Joint as far as Winteringham and there to invest in port facilities. The Trent was to be dealt with by a bridge 385 yards in length including two swing spans. A Board of Trade inspector found the bridge proposal impractical and the Bill was withdrawn. These seemingly hopeless threats had persuaded the Great Central to tighten its grip on the North Lindsey Light Railway. With Great Central support, the North Lindsey obtained powers in 1906 to extend west via Whitton to Alkborough and east to Barton on Humber.

Fearing that North Lindsey shareholders might be receptive to an offer from the L&Y, the Great Central arranged for its own working agreement to be ratified by Act of Parliament. The North Lindsey acquiesced in this, having obtained a Great Central promise that the Alkborough and Barton lines would go ahead.

In the event, the only extension was the 2½ miles to Whitton, opened on 1 December 1910. This brought the Railway close to the steamer pier, built in 1865, which was a calling point for the Gainsborough & Hull and Goole & Hull Steam Packet Companies. These sailings stopped during the First

A Gainsborough & Hull paddle steamer calls at Whitton Pier, where the North Lindsey hoped to pick up interchange traffic. *(Martin Bairstow collection)*

World War and the pier was demolished about 1920.

The train service to Whitton was never more than twice a day. By 1922, there were only two departures from Scunthorpe, at 7.55am for Winteringham and 1.20pm to Whitton with a third train on Saturdays only at 6.00pm as far as Winteringham. On 13 July 1925, the line closed to passengers. Goods traffic continued until 11 October 1951 when the line was closed beyond West Halton. It was cut back further on 29 May 1961 when Winterton & Thealby again became the terminus. That closed to goods traffic on 20 July 1964, leaving Roxby Mines as the limit of rail operation.

At its southern end, the fortunes of the branch took a very different course. Normanby Park steelworks began production in 1912. It was the creation of John Lysaght Ltd, of Bristol, who were drawn to the Normanby site by the proximity of ore deposits and by the recently opened branch railway. A public goods station was opened at Normanby on 1 August 1912 and access to the light railway was improved by a new ½ mile curve off the main line which avoided the need to negotiate Frodingham goods yard. The Great Central planned to double the track between Scunthorpe and Normanby but the First World War intervened and the scheme had to await the LNER Scunthorpe area improvements in the late 1920s.

The Normanby private rail system fed into Dragonby Sidings, alongside the North Lindsey Light Railway. Normanby Park North and South boxes controlled access to each end of the sidings. In 1938, Lysaghts commissioned Flixborough Wharf on the Trent, to which their private railway was extended.

Private industrial locos and wagons worked over the North Lindsey Light Railway. Crosby Mines signal box was claimed to be the busiest on British Railways for controlling non BR industrial traffic. Iron ore was brought from the mines near Winterton, both to Normanby Park and to the works at Appleby - Frodingham and Redbourne Hill which stood to the south of Scunthorpe. To accommodate this latter movement, the "common user line" or "ore branch" was built parallel to the Light Railway, passing underneath the Great Central Main Line. In BR days, this route was used to carry hot metal (liquid iron) in "torpedo" cars between the different steel plants. Normanby Park Works closed in the early 1980s, since when steel production has been concentrated on the Appleby - Frodingham complex, south of the main line.

The North Lindsey Light Railway survives as a single track from Trent Junction to Roxby where, since 1993, trainloads of Greater Manchester's household waste have been tipped into the former mine workings. The North Lincolnshire Local Plan envisages conversion to a cycle way when tipping is eventually finished.

The southern half of the Light Railway gained a prosperity which evaded the northern reach. At Normanby Park North, an O4 on pilot duty passes a United Steel Co "Janus" diesel on ironstone empties. *(John Oxley)*

The platform side of Whitton Station building.
(Martin Bairstow collection)

Winterton & Thealby Station after the track was lifted.
(John Oxley)

When the North Lindsey Light Railway had a passenger service, it ran from this small station, just on the branch. Never from Frodingham Station.
(Martin Bairstow collection)

Conditions of Carriage

Peter Sunderland has kindly loaned a facsimile copy of the Great Central 1903 Summer timetable. The train times themselves could just as easily be found in "Bradshaw". What makes this publication interesting is the wealth of incidental information.

There are fares and charges for every conceivable item that you might be tempted to dispatch by rail. There are commercial announcements soliciting custom for the Great Central, together with warnings and disclaimers trying to make sure that the Railway does not end up liable for any mishap.

Eight pages are devoted to a list of fares to almost every station in the British Isles, which could conceivably be reached from London Marylebone. In almost all cases, fares are quoted for first and third class, the former being more than 50% greater than the latter. To most destinations, but not Hull Corporation Pier, a price is quoted for a horse, usually at three times the third class fare and for a carriage at anything from the same as a horse to 50% more. Right up to the 1960s, the working timetable specified trains, usually expresses, to which a horse box or a flat wagon for a carriage could not be attached. In theory, you could request one on any other train and you only had to pay the published fare. In practice, the facility must have become very rare by the time it was abolished.

2½ pages of the 1903 timetable are devoted to Market Day tickets, which generally give a 25% discount on the return fare, third class. Availability was limited to specific days and sometimes restricted to certain trains.

Market Day at Barton on Humber was Monday, with special tickets available from Barnetby, Brigg, New Holland and Ulceby. Of much greater significance was Market Day in Brigg on Thursday for which tickets were issued from most stations in North Lincolnshire and from as far afield as Hull, Doncaster and Sheffield. There was an extra train to Brigg at 9.50am from Cleethorpes and 9.56 from New Holland Pier, the two combining at Brocklesby. Return was by normal service from Brigg but a Thursdays only connection was required at 4.35 from New Holland Town to Barton to avoid a long wait.

On Tuesdays and Fridays, Market Day tickets were issued to Hull Corporation Pier from all over North Lincolnshire. From every starting point, there was the option of paying 3d return extra for first class on the ferry.

Passengers to and from Market Towns, whether or not on special tickets, could carry with them free of charge, goods for purchase or sale, excluding furniture or musical instruments, up to a weight of 60 lbs (third class) or 120lbs (first class). The ordinary free luggage allowance was 100lbs (third class) or 150lbs (first class) but this excluded goods or merchandise. It is not clear whether the Market Day allowance was extra to the ordinary one. Excess luggage was chargeable on a most complicated scale, which was halved for commercial travellers, musicians, certain other entertainers and seafarers. It says in bold type that excess luggage charges will be strictly enforced. Goodness knows how.

Workmen's Tickets are covered only by a general advertisement. Under the Cheap Trains Act, 1883, Companies had to provide minimum facilities for workmen to travel at affordable prices, generally return for the normal cost of a single. Workmen were not defined except by the time of trains to which these tickets were limited. The Board of Trade could arbitrate if the arrangements fell short of the spirit of the legislation. In practice, most Railways began to look upon workmen as a bulk traffic, rather than a statutory nuisance and provided more than the minimum service.

The Great Central was keen that customers should know how to contact its principal officers and agents. Only a few telephone numbers are quoted. The chief method of fast communication was by telegram. As these were charged by the word, it made sense to have an abbreviated address, which was recognised by the Post Office. Some individuals and businesses tried to define themselves through a personalised telegraphic address.

The General Manager, Sam Fay, was "Fay Great Central Manchester". The Engineer was "Viaduct Manchester" and the Accountant "Ledger Manchester". The Mineral Manager was "Coalpit Manchester" and the Cattle Inspector "Quadruped Liverpool".

The travel agents Dean & Dawson could be contacted at "Excursions Sheffield", "Excursions Nottingham" or the more exotic sounding "Viaggio London" or "Viaggio Paris". This concern, with 26 branch offices, was owned by the Great Central from 1904.

Also owned by the Railway, but trading in its own name was Thompson Mckay & Co Ltd. This firm had served as cartage agents for the MS&L in Manchester since the 1850s. In 1869 they were trusted with the cartage business in other towns, including Hull and Grimsby, and were taken into Railway ownership in 1887. They could be contacted at "Envoy Hull", "Envoy Manchester" but "Speed Leeds".

Grimsby is not mentioned in this context, but "Royal Grimsby" would find you the Manager of the Royal Hotel. Not that you would need to pay for a telegram to reserve a room in a Great Central Hotel as any Station Master would send it free of charge.

Whatever the method of communication, the timetable promises that "all goods and enquiries will receive the most careful and prompt attention" from the Companies representatives and agents, who are listed both for the areas directly served by the Great Central and for the rest of the Country including Ireland and the Channel Isles.

There is frequent reference in the timetable to "an Act passed in 1830 for the more effectual protection of the Mail Contractors, Stage Coach

Proprietors, and other Common Carriers for Hire, against the loss of, or injury to, Parcels or Packages delivered to them for conveyance or custody, the value of which shall not be declared to them by the owners thereof". If this Act had a short title, it is not quoted.

Under this protection, the Railway requires the contents of packages to be declared and, if the value is more than £10, an insurance fee to be paid. For this there is a scale of charges, based on four classes of goods. Class One includes money, postage stamps, clocks, trinkets, title deeds and books. The charge is 1/2000 of the declared value, irrespective of distance to any station in Great Britain, including the Isle of Wight. The charge is trebled to other off shore islands or to a seaport in Ireland and quadrupled to an internal station in Ireland.

Class Two goods, at double the Class One rate, are mainly jewellery. Class Three, at five times Class One, are pictures and paintings. Class Four, at ten times, is mainly glass. So a consignment of glass to a station in Ireland would have to be insured at 2% of its value. Naturally, the Insurance Company had the right of inspection before acceptance. The arrangements applied equally to goods and passenger trains.

If packages were consigned to a station "To Be Called For", the Railway cited statutory authority for declining liability for items not collected. In the case of Fruit, Fish, Meat, Poultry, Game and other perishable articles, the time limit for collection was fixed at six hours after arrival.

Except under special contract, dangerous goods were not accepted at all. These included Gunpowder, Aquafortis, Oil of Vitriol, Spirits of Salt, Corrosive Acids, and Lucifer or Congreve Matches. These items were proscribed by the Railway Clauses Consolidation Act 1845, to which reference is made in a section of the timetable listing the various offences for which persons could be fined. This particular offence carried a maximum penalty of £20 (ten weeks wage for a skilled worker and a years pay for some people). Most other penalties were set at £5 or £2, the latter always expressed as 40 shillings.

Prominent on the £5 tariff was "making use, without reasonable and sufficient cause, of the Means of Communication between the Passengers and the Servants of the Company in charge of a Train", that is pulling the communication cord. £2 offences included taking a dog into a passenger compartment, travelling with an infectious disorder or persisting in entering a carriage or compartment which already contains the full number of persons which it was constructed to convey. It was, and still is, an offence to pass the return half of a ticket to somebody else. It is doubtless still an offence to travel on the Roof, Steps or Footboard of any carriage, though the fact doesn't receive much publicity nowadays. A topic, still with us, is the offence of travelling in a superior class to that for which the ticket was issued. This was also a Forty Shilling penalty but the Bye law does allow the defence of no intent to defraud.

A rather impractical bye law is that governing the situation where a train arrives at an intermediate station and finds more people wanting to board than there is room. Priority is given to those travelling the furthest distance and, in the event of a tie, to those who bought their tickets earliest as evidenced by the serial numbers. If, to relieve the situation, a passenger opts to travel in an inferior class to that for which he has paid, he will be refunded the difference provided he makes an application prior to departure of the train. The Company accepts no responsibility for these rules actually being enforced.

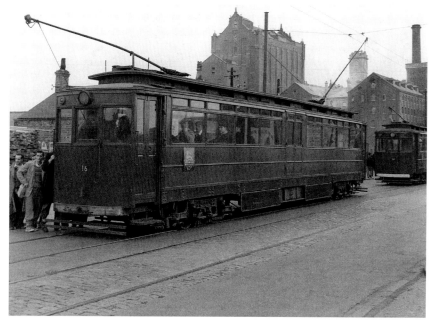

Who would have checked the serial numbers on the tickets, in the event that these fellows had exceeded the available seating capacity? 16 and 14 at Corporation Bridge on 25 September 1955.

(J C W Halliday)

The Axholme Joint Railway

An LMS owned Sentinel steam car ran on the Axholme Joint for a month during Summer 1926. In December 1930, the line acquired its own Sentinel car. It appeared in the green and cream livery used on LNER railcars. It carried the number 44 and was lettered Axholme Joint Railway. It is seen leaving Reedness Junction for Goole.
(Martin Bairstow Collection)

The Isle of Axholme is an area of Lincolnshire, bounded by the Rivers Trent, Don, Idle and Torne. Immediately to the north is a corner of Yorkshire, known as the Marshland. The combined area is one of good agricultural land, which by 1900, had still to be penetrated by railways.

The Light Railways Act 1896 was intended to make it easier to promote lines in such areas. The Goole & Marshland Light Railway was authorised in August 1898 to run 13¾ miles from Marshland Junction, south of Goole, to Fockerby. Work began straight away and the line was opened for goods as far as Reedness Junction on 8 January 1900.

In March 1899, an Order was made for the Isle of Axholme Light Railway, 22 miles in length, which was to start from Reedness Junction on the Goole & Marshland and reach the Great Northern/ Great Eastern Joint Line at Haxey Junction, north of Gainsborough.

The two light railways might or might not have been completed as independent concerns. The question was never put to the test. By an Act of July 1902, the North Eastern and Lancashire & Yorkshire Railways absorbed both concerns jointly.

Now known as the Axholme Joint, the system was completed over the next two and a half years. Fockerby and Crowle both opened to all traffic on 10 August 1903, with a passenger service from Goole. Fockerby might have been the starting point for an extension tunnelling under the Trent to try and attack the steel traffic at Scunthorpe. Nothing ever came of this except that the threat encouraged the Great Central into supporting the North Lindsey Light Railway.

The extension from Crowle to Haxey opened to goods on 14 November 1904 and to passengers on 2 January 1905. This last section included three substantial engineering features. The largest carried the Axholme Joint over the Great Central Railway and the Keadby Canal. It comprised three brick arches, then the girder spanning the GC, followed by a single brick arch over the tow path then the swing bridge over the canal and final brick arch, beyond which was the signal box. The whole structure was built wide enough for double track. In the absence of an electric power supply, the swing bridge was oil powered. In the early days, it might be opened a dozen times a day for benefit of canal traffic with masts or high funnels. The Railway tried but never succeeded in gaining authority to have it welded shut. Rail traffic was always subject to a 10 mph restriction.

A short way to the South, the railway crossed the New Thorn and Double Rivers and the main road by a 12 arch brick viaduct. Then a nine arch viaduct carried the line over two drains and a farm track. Both these structures were wide enough for double track.

The 5 mile branch from Epworth to Hatfield Moor had been included in the 1899 Order. It was not proceeded with at that stage and powers had to be renewed in 1905. It opened to goods on 1 March 1909, but never had a passenger service. An 8 mile extension to Black Carr, near Doncaster was authorised in 1909. Extensions of time were obtained but the First World War intervened before work had started.

The two main line Companies had been drawn in by the prospect of coal coming into Haxey from collieries in the Tickhill area, south of Doncaster. A Light Railway Order was issued in 1901 for a line from Tickhill to Haxey, but this was never built. Instead, the Great Northern built a line from Bawtry to Haxey over part of the proposed route, opening in 1912. Tickhill was served from 1909 by the South Yorkshire Joint Railway, in which the NE and L&Y both had an interest.

Heavy coal traffic never did use the Axholme Joint, which remained a rural byway. The passenger service comprised three trains each way between

Goole and Haxey Junction, only two of which had connections from Reedness to Fockerby. There were two extra trains on Saturdays but nothing on Sundays.

The passenger service ended on 15 July 1933, though some excursions ran after that. Parcels and luggage in advance were still accepted for carriage on the pick up goods. From the beginning until the late 1940s, the regular goods engines were Barton Wright 0-6-0s from Goole Shed, including No 957 (52044) which is preserved on the Keighley & Worth Valley Railway.

Complete closure took place south of Epworth on 1 February 1956, though the section was used for wagon storage until lifted about 1962. The Hatfield Moor branch followed on 30 September 1963. The remainder of the system was closed to public traffic from 5 April 1965. On Thursday 1 April, a four coach DMU had conveyed a party of school children from Goole to Fockerby, Epworth and back.

For the next seven years, the line was retained as a "long siding" between Marshland Junction and Belton for the sole purpose of conveying occasional heavy loads to and from Keadby Power Station. Large transformers were loaded at Belton Station and conveyed by rail to Ealand, near Crowle Town because there was no way that such loads could cross the Keadby Canal by road, nor could they approach from any other direction. But on 5 May 1972, the new road bridge opened just west of Crowle Central Station, replacing the small swing bridge over the canal and adjacent level crossing on the Doncaster to Scunthorpe line. That was the end of this lease of life for the Axholme Joint Railway.

The track was soon lifted and the large swing bridge dismantled. The 12 "Crowle Arches" were demolished with explosives in Autumn 1981 so as to relieve a bottle neck on the A18 where lorries had been obliged to drive in the middle of the road to get under. The nearby nine arch viaduct is still standing.

Crowle, Belton and Epworth are all significant communities, with potential for commuting to Doncaster and Scunthorpe. In terms of passengers, the downfall of the Axholme Joint was that it ran north - south when the traffic is east - west.

The Sentinel railcar calls at Crowle Joint Station with its very low platforms. The view is looking north. The station buildings are behind the camera.
(Martin Bairstow collection)

The power unit end of the railcar, again at Crowle, looking south.
(Martin Bairstow collection)

Eastoft Station, looking towards Reedness in April 1965. The very low platform is just visible by the wooden building.   *(R J Goodman)*

Reedness Junction with the Sentinel car in the Crowle platform. Fockerby branch to the left, cattle wagons in the siding.

(Martin Bairstow collection)

Crowle Swing Bridge, still serviceable for the very occasional power station traffic in June 1968. A class 47 on the GC line heads towards Scunthorpe.   *(John Marshall)*

Present Day Passenger Services

The hourly "Trans Pennine Express" runs from Cleethorpes to Manchester Airport, serving Grimsby Town, Barnetby, Scunthorpe, Doncaster, Meadowhall, Sheffield, Stockport, and Manchester Piccadilly. Some trains call at Habrough. The service is worked by two car class 158 Diesel Multiple Units and has functioned in the present form since May 1992, though the extension to Manchester Airport did not begin until 1995.

West of Scunthorpe, there is an hourly local service calling at all stations to Sheffield, following the same route as the "Trans Pennine" apart from the detour to serve Rotherham.

Nine trains per day link Cleethorpes with Barton on Humber serving all stations, New Clee by request only. The timetable has hardly changed since 1985, except that the Sunday service has been Summer Only in recent years.

There are nine trains a day, not at regular intervals, between Grimsby Town and Lincoln Central, serving Habrough, Barnetby and Market Rasen. The first and last of the day begin at Cleethorpes. All but the last two go through to Newark North Gate, where there are connections for London.

Lincoln Central is the terminus of an hourly local service from Sheffield. Frequency between Gainsborough Lea Road, Saxilby and Lincoln is enhanced by the handful of trains, which come via the "Joint Line" from Doncaster.

There are no published plans for any service enhancements. There has been speculation that Hull Trains might repeat its apparent success on North Humberside and restore through London trains to Lincoln, Grimsby and Cleethorpes. Our contact in First Group suggests that further expansion of Hull Trains will take the form of more trains to Hull, including stops at Retford, which would fill gaps in the present Main Line service there. Any long term ambitions south of the Humber might only be as far as Lincoln, with Grimsby and Cleethorpes a very distant thought. We don't know whether a London to Lincoln service would be via Newark North Gate or via Peterborough, Spalding and Sleaford.

156 484 has arrived at Scunthorpe on the hourly all stations from Sheffield. 15 May 2004. *(Martin Bairstow)*

158 773 passing Althorpe in March 1997 *(Stuart Baker)*

The Lincolnshire Coast Light Railway

"Jurassic" running round at North Sea Lane during its last steaming at August Bank Holiday 1985.
(Chris Bates)

The Lincolnshire Coast Light Railway claims to be the only true narrow gauge railway (as distinct from a miniature railway) on the East Coast. It is now based in the Skegness Water Leisure Park but, at the time of writing, has not yet reopened. For 25 years, the 60 cm (1ft 11½ in) gauge line was a distinctive part of North Lincolnshire's railways at Humberston, south of Cleethorpes. It created a unique and historically important collection of early English narrow gauge railway carriages and wagons, diesel and steam locomotives.

The line transported holidaymakers from a bus terminus (and latterly, a Sunday market) to the Fitties Holiday Camp and to Humberston Beach. Its origins lay in Lincolnshire's once extensive network of narrow gauge railways, which served the potato growing and brick-making industries. The largest was the Nocton Estates Light Railway, seven miles south of Lincoln. Track and rolling stock came from the trench railways built by the British military in the First World War to take troops and munitions to the front lines. When the Nocton system was due for replacement by improved roads, a pioneering group of North Lincolnshire railway enthusiasts decided to preserve some of the equipment and convert it for use on a passenger carrying line. To achieve this, they built the LCLR. The first half mile line opened on 26 August 1960 from North Sea Lane to Beach

Halt (for the Humberston Fitties Holiday Camp). By the following year, annual traffic had risen to 60,000 passengers. This prompted Grimsby - Cleethorpes Transport to compete with a mini-bus service which, starting from the terminus for routes from Grimsby and Cleethorpes, took two-thirds of the Railway's traffic.

In 1966, the lease expired and Grimsby Rural District Council asked for return of the land upon which the line ran, for camping development. The LCLR moved to a new alignment, parallel to the original, about 50 yards to the south. At the same time, the line was extended to South Sea Lane. The change over took place on 15 August 1966. The new railway was one mile in length. There were two intermediate halts, Beach and St Anthonys, used intermittently.

The Railway closed at the end of August 1985, a victim of social and economic changes affecting the holiday industry. The hope was to relocate and rebuild the Railway and a site has been found at Skegness, where work continues.

LCLR passengers were often conveyed in one or two open coaches, converted from War Department class D bogie wagons. There was also some enclosed stock, including two large bogie carriages built by the Gloucester Rail, Carriage and Wagon Company in 1924 for the Ashover Light Railway.

These were restored from static sports pavilions to re-enter traffic in 1962 and 1963. The sole passenger coach from the Sand Hutton Light Railway was also restored and returned to service on the LCLR. The unique passenger carriage from the Nocton Estates Light Railway, used for inspections of the estates and shooting parties, was purchased by the LCLR in 1982 but never put into traffic.

Services were usually powered by one of the fleet of Simplex (Motor Rail) diesels: the initial one, "Paul", was built in 1926 (works number 3995) and was given a new all over metal body when purchased by the LCLR. Four of the five diesel locomotives were Simplexes: "Wilton" (works number 7481, built 1940) acquired from Humberston Brickworks; "Nocton" (works number 1935, built 1920); "Major" (works number 8622, built 1944) and an unnamed example, (works number 8874, also from 1944). A Ruston & Hornsby diesel of 1933 vintage from Southam Lime Works in Warwickshire,

was scrapped soon after arrival although some components went to the Tal-y-llyn Railway.

The steam locomotive "Jurassic", purchased by the LCLR in 1961, was popular with enthusiasts and travellers but was only used intermittently. It is an 0-6-0 saddle tank built in 1903 by Peckett & Sons (works number 1008) for Southam Lime Works.

Four vehicles, initially owned by the LCLR, have been purchased by the LCLR Historic Vehicles Trust. Their importance has been recognised by the Science Museum and the Transport Trust who contributed to the cost of restoration. For many years they were displayed in the Museum of Army Transport, near Beverley but are now on the new LCLR site at Skegness. They include the only surviving ambulance van built for the WW1 trench railways, two Class D bogie wagons and a Class P four-wheeled ration wagon.

The LCLR Historic Vehicle Trust may be contacted at 12 Giles Street, Cleethorpes DN35 8EA.

The former Ashover Light Railway coach was fitted with seats recovered from Liverpool tramcars. The date is September 1963, when daily services ran to the end of the month. Just visible in the cab of the Simplex diesel loco is the 15 year old driver, name of Bates. *(Chris Bates collection)*

Seagull's eye view as "Jurassic" steams out of North Sea Lane on a damp and dreary Sunday in August 1985. *(Chris Bates)*

The Cleethorpes Coast Light Railway

Arriving at Kingsway Station in July 2004. No 1 "Sutton Belle" in the other platform. Sandy River No24 the train engine.
(Chris Bates)

The mile long 15in gauge line is the latest and most successful manifestation of the miniature railways, which have operated on the seafront at Cleethorpes since 1948.

The builders of the original 10¼in gauge line sold it to Arthur Clethro of Scarborough in 1954. Pictures from those days show at work, scaled down versions of GNR Atlantics, a GWR Castle, an LNER A3 and an LMS or Irish outline 4 - 6 - 0. In 1959, the line was bought by Cleethorpes Borough Council, who operated it as two single tracks, each with a diesel outline loco reminiscent of the pioneering LMS 10000 or 10001, working push - pull from stations at the Boating Lake and Thurnscoe.

By 1971, lack of investment and maintenance meant that the line was life expired. The following year, the Council rebuilt and extended it to the previously unknown gauge of 14¼in, operated by Severn-Lamb propane powered steam outline locos.

In 1991, the line was bought by the present owner and managing director, Chris Shaw, and reguaged to 15in. It has since been extended across the boating lake by an impressive brick viaduct to a new overall roofed terminus at Kingsway, with a further extension at Lakeside. There are plans to extend a further 1¼ miles south into Humberston using part of the track bed of the erstwhile Lincolnshire Coast Light Railway.

A quarter scale LNER class A3 by the boating lake in 1949.
(Chris Bates collection)

There are now around 15 steam and diesel locos and 30 carriages. In 2002, the line won the Heritage Railways Association Small Groups Award "for exemplifying the historic importance of seaside and miniature railways with particular benefit to the resort of Cleethorpes and for preserving in its entirety the historically important Sutton Coldfield Miniature Railway Collection"

The latter collection was purchased by the line's Supporters Association, and by some individual members, with help from the National Heritage Memorial Fund. It consists of two 4 - 4 - 2 steam engines, "Sutton Belle" and "Sutton Flyer", a petrol mechanical railcar modelled on a GWR "Flying Banana", four open and six closed carriages together with steel work from the main station roof, an engine shed and signal box.

The Railway operates at weekends and school holidays throughout the year, though in 2004, there was no service during November.

Waiting for the train, Summer 1949.
(Chris Bates collection)

The Wonderland Miniature Railway

There was for many years also a 7¼in gauge line under the Big Dipper at the Wonderland amusement park adjacent to the BR tracks on Cleethorpes seafront. The little line is held in fond memory by many people in the area, as an appeal for information in the Grimsby Telegraph has proved, with many calls offering information. The railway was always steam operated, with anthracite fired locomotives.

Geoff Goodman, of Cleethorpes, helped construct the track in 1953 for East Coast Amusements Ltd, the owners of Wonderland. He recalls that the rails were held together with linking plates. The first two locomotives, "Henrietta" and "Grimsby Town" were built in the Company's workshop and featured in the December 1959 edition of *The Model Engineer.* It is believed that eight locomotives were eventually based on the line, three of which survive on a private railway in Coniston, together with rolling stock. These are an American styled Pacific, 4 - 6 - 4 "Henrietta" and a model of "The Flying Scotsman". CCLR supporter Ray Chrome recalls that the track was ¼ mile long and that there were also two "Royal Scot" models, one with smoke deflectors and one without, and a Bassett Lowke loco which was not popular with drivers. The carriages held 54 seats. Six old pence would buy riders two circuits. Services began at 10.00 and would continue until 22.30.

Former Wonderland worker, Frank Priest says that part of the fascination lay with the fact that the line was oval shaped, fully signalled and crossed over a lake. It was engineered to a high degree, as was all the Wonderland complex. The line closed about 1970. The family who owned Wonderland, Reuben and Bessie Felyce and their son Toby are all now deceased. Jim Smith, a volunteer on the Lincolnshire Coast Light Railway, says that as a child he preferred the Wonderland Railway to the Big Dipper!

The Big Dipper at Cleethorpes, with "Director" class D11 No 62660 "Butler Henderson" in the carriage sidings.
(John Oxley)

Appendices

The Manchester, Sheffield & Lincolnshire Main Line

Opened		Miles	Stations	Opened	Closed
01/03/1848	Habrough - Grimsby Town	0	Retford	17/07/1849	
01/11/1848	Brigg - Habrough	6¼	Sturton	17/07/1849	31/10/1959
02/04/1849	Gainsborough Central - Brigg	10¼	Gainsborough Central	02/04/1849	
17/07/1849	Retford - Gainsborough Central	14¾	Blyton	02/04/1849	31/01/1959
		17¾	Northorpe	02/04/1849	02/07/1955
		20½	Kirton Lindsey	02/04/1849	
		24	Scawby & Hibaldstow	02/04/1849	03/02/1968
		26¾	Brigg	01/11/1848	
		30½	Barnetby	01/11/1848	
		35¼	Brocklesby	01/11/1848	
		37	Habrough	01/03/1848	
		40¾	Stallingborough	01/03/1848	
		41¾	Healing	01/04/1881	
		43	Great Coates	01/03/1848	
		45	Grimsby Town	01/03/1848	
		46	Grimsby Docks	01/08/1853	
		46¼	Riby Street	01/10/1904	14/04/1941
		46¾	New Clee	01/07/1875	
		48¼	Cleethorpes	06/04/1863	

New Holland to Barton, Immingham and Habrough

Opened		Miles	Stations	Opened	Closed
01/03/1848	New Holland Pier - Habrough	0	New Holland Pier	01/03/1848	24/06/1981
01/03/1849	New Holland Pier - Barton on Humber	¼	New Holland Town	01/03/1848	
29/06/1910	Ulceby - Immingham Dock	1¼	Barrow Haven	08/04/1850	
01/10/1910	Killingholme - Immingham Dock (goods)	3¼	Barton on Humber	01/03/1849	
01/05/1911	Goxhill - Immingham Dock (all traffic)	2¼	Goxhill	01/03/1848	
		5¼	East Halton	01/05/1911	15/06/1963
Closed		6¾	Admiralty Platform	By 1930	15/06/1963
15/06/1963	Goxhill - Immingham Dock (passenger)	8	Killingholme	01/05/1911	15/06/1963
15/06/1963	Goxhill - Killingholme (all traffic)	10	Immingham Dock	01/05/1911	04/10/1969
04/10/1969	Ulceby - Immingham Dock (passenger)	3¾	Thornton Abbey	01/08/1849	
24/06/1981	New Holland Pier	6¼	Ulceby	01/03/1849	
		8	Habrough	01/03/1849	

Trent, Ancholme & Grimsby

Opened		Miles	Stations	Opened	Closed
11/12/1855	Doncaster - Thorne (goods)	0	Doncaster	07/09/1848	
01/07/1856	Doncaster - Thorne (passenger)	4	Kirk Sandall	03/05/1991	
10/09/1859	Thorne - Keadby	4¾	Barnby Dun	01/07/1856	02/09/1967
01/05/1866	Keadby Junction - Barnetby (goods)	7	Stainforth & Hatfield	01/07/1856	
01/10/1866	Keadby Junction - Barnetby (passenger)	10	Thorne South	01/07/1856	
		11½	Mauds Bridge	01/11/1859	30/09/1866
		13½	Medge Hall	01/11/1859	10/09/1960
		14½	Godnow Bridge	01/11/1859	31/03/1917
		16	Crowle Central	10/09/1859	
		–	Keadby	10/09/1859	31/10/1874
		19¾	Althorpe	01/10/1866	
		20	Gunness & B	01/09/1869	21/05/1916
		23¾	Scunthorpe & F	11/03/1928	
		24	Frodingham & S	01/10/1866	10/03/1928
		27¼	Appleby (Lincs)	01/10/1866	03/06/1967
		31¾	Elsham	01/10/1866	02/10/1993
		34½	Barnetby	01/11/1848	

Retford - Lincoln - Barnetby

Opened		Miles	Stations	Opened	Closed
01/11/1848	Market Rasen - Barnetby	0	Retford	17/07/1849	
18/12/1848	Lincoln Midland - Market Rasen	5½	Leverton	01/12/1850	01/11/1959
09/04/1849	Gainsborough Trent Jn - Lincoln Cen.	8	Cottam	01/12/1850	01/11/1959
07/08/1850	Clarborough Junction - Sykes Jun.	9½	Torksey	01/12/1850	01/11/1959
		13¾	Saxilby	09/04/1849	
Closed temporarily		16¼	Skellingthorpe	02/01/1865	31/05/1868
30/11/1864	Gainsborough Trent Jn - Sykes Jn	19½	Lincoln Central	17/10/1848	
		0	Lincoln St Marks	03/08/1846	11/05/1985
Reopened		5	Reepham (Lincs)	18/12/1848	30/10/1965
15/07/1867	Gainsborough Trent Jn - Sykes Jn	6½	Langworth	18/12/1848	30/10/1965
		9¾	Snelland	18/12/1848	30/10/1965
Closed		11⅛	Wickenby	18/12/1848	30/10/1965
01/11/1959	Clarborough Junction - Sykes Junction	15¼	Market Rasen	01/11/1848	
		18	Claxby & Usselby	01/11/1848	05/03/1960
Reopened to goods		20¾	Holton le Moor	01/11/1848	30/10/1965
31/01/1966	Torksey - Sykes Junction	22¼	Moortown for Caistor	01/11/1848	30/10/1965
1968	Clarborough Junction - Cottam	23¾	North Kelsey	01/11/1848	30/10/1965
		25¾	Howsham	01/11/1848	30/10/1965
Closed again		28	Bigby Road	01/03/1852	30/09/1882
18/09/1988	Torksey - Sykes Junction	29¾	Barnetby	01/11/1848	
		0	Gainsborough Lea Rd	15/07/1867	
		2¼	Lea	01/08/1849	05/08/1957
		5	Stow Park	09/04/1849	10/09/1961

North Lindsey Light Railway

Opened		Miles	Stations	Opened	Closed
03/09/1906	Scunthorpe - West Halton (goods)	0	Scunthorpe	03/09/1906	13/07/1925
03/09/1906	Scunthorpe - Winterton & T (passenger)	5	Winterton & Thealby	03/09/1906	13/07/1925
15/07/1907	Winterton & T - Winteringham	6	West Halton	15/07/1907	13/07/1925
01/12/1907	Winteringham - Whitton	8½	Winteringham	15/07/1907	13/07/1925
Closed		11	Whitton	01/12/1910	13/07/1925
13/07/1925	Passenger throughout				
11/10/1951	West Halton - Whitton (goods)				
29/05/1961	Winterton & T - West Halton (goods)				
20/07/1964	Roxby Mines - Winterton & T (goods)				

Axholme Joint

Opened		Miles	Stations	Opened	Closed
10/08/1903	Marshland Junction - Crowle Joint	0	Goole	29/03/1848	
10/08/1903	Reedness Junction - Fockerby	5¾	Reedness Junction	10/08/1903	15/07/1933
14/11/1904	Crowle Joint - Haxey Junction (goods)	8¾	Eastoft	10/08/1903	15/07/1933
02/01/1905	Crowle Joint - Haxey Junction (passr)	10	Luddington	10/08/1903	15/07/1933
01/03/1909	Epworth - Hatfield Moor (goods)	11¼	Fockerby	10/08/1903	15/07/1933
Closed		8¾	Crowle Joint	10/08/1903	15/07/1933
15/07/1933	Passenger throughout	13	Belton	02/01/1905	15/07/1933
01/02/1956	Epworth - Haxey Junction (goods)	14¾	Epworth	02/01/1905	15/07/1933
30/09/1963	Epworth - Hatfield Moor (goods)	17¾	Haxey Town	02/01/1905	15/07/1933
05/04/1965	Reedness Junction - Fockerby (goods)	19½	Haxey Junction	02/01/1905	15/07/1933
05/04/1965	Belton - Epworth (goods)				
05/05/1972	Marshland Jn - Belton (all traffic)				